ENTER HIS COURTS WITH PRAISE

ENTER HIS COURTS WITH PRAISE

A Study of the Role of Music and the Arts in Worship

Robert E. Webber

The Alleluia! Series of the Institute for Worship Studies

HENDRICKSON PUBLISHERS

Hendrickson Publishers, Inc.
P. O. Box 3473
Peabody, Massachusetts 01961-3473

ENTER HIS COURTS WITH PRAISE:
A Study of the Role of Music and the Arts in Worship
by Robert E. Webber

ISBN 1-56563-275-3

First printing, November 1997

Printed in the United States of America

CONTENTS

CONCLUSION

WELCOME TO THE ALLELUIA! SERIES

This Bible study series has been designed by the Institute for Worship Studies primarily for laypersons in the church.

We are living in a time when worship has become a distinct priority for the church. For years, the church has emphasized evangelism, teaching, fellowship, missions, and service to society to the neglect of the very source of its power—worship. But in recent years we have witnessed a Spirit-led renewal in the study and practice of worship.

Because worship has been neglected for so many years, there is precious little information and teaching on the subject in our seminaries, Bible schools, and local churches.

The mission of the Institute for Worship Studies is to make the study of worship available to everyone in the church—academician, pastor, worship leader, music minister, and layperson.

Laypersons will find the seven courses of the Alleluia! Series to be inspiring, informative, and life changing. Each course of study is rooted in biblical teaching, draws from the rich historical treasures of the church, and is highly practical and accessible.

The Institute for Worship Studies presents this course, *Enter His Courts with Praise: A Study of the Role of Music and the Arts in Worship,* as a service to the local church and to its ministry of worship to God. May this study warm your heart, inform your mind, and kindle your spirit. May it inspire and set on fire the worship of the local church. And may this study minister to the church and to the One, Holy, Triune God in whose name it is offered.

THE SEVEN COURSES IN THE ALLELUIA! WORSHIP SERIES

Learning to Worship with All Your Heart: A Study in the Biblical Foundations of Worship

You are led into the rich teachings of worship in both the Old and the New Testaments. Learn the vocabulary of worship, be introduced to theological themes, and study various descriptions of worship. Each lesson inspires you to worship at a deeper level—from the inside out.

Rediscovering the Missing Jewel: A Study of Worship through the Centuries
This stretching course introduces you to the actual worship styles of Christians in other centuries and geographical locations. Study the history of the early, medieval, Reformation, modern, and contemporary periods of worship. Learn from them how your worship today may be enriched, inspired, and renewed. Each lesson introduces you to rich treasures of worship adaptable for contemporary use.

Renew Your Worship! A Study in the Blending of Traditional and Contemporary Worship
This inspiring course leads you into a deeper understanding and experience of your Sunday worship. How does worship bring the congregation into the presence of God, mold the people by the Word, and feed the believers spiritually? The answer to these and other questions will bring a new spiritual depth to your experience of worship.

Enter His Courts with Praise: A Study of the Role of Music and the Arts in Worship
This course introduces you to the powerful way the arts can communicate the mystery of God at work in worship. Music, visual arts, drama, dance, and mime are seen as means through which the gospel challenges the congregation and changes lives.

Rediscovering the Christian Feasts: A Study in the Services of the Christian Year
This stimulating and stretching course helps you experience the traditional church calendar with new eyes. It challenges the secular concept of time and shows how the practice of the Christian year offers an alternative to secularism and shapes the Christian's day-to-day experience of time, using the gospel as its grid.

Encountering the Healing Power of God: A Study in the Sacred Actions of Worship
This course makes a powerful plea for the recovery of those sacred actions that shape the spiritual life. Baptism, Communion, anointing with oil, and other sacred actions are all interpreted with reflection on the death and resurrection of Jesus. These actions shape the believer's spiritual experience into a continual pattern of death to sin and rising to life in the Spirit.

Empowered by the Holy Spirit: A Study in the Ministries of Worship
This course will challenge you to see the relationship between worship and life in the secular world. It empowers the believer in evangelism, spiritual formation, social action, care ministries, and other acts of love and charity.

Take all seven courses and earn a Certificate of Worship Studies (CWS). For more information, call the Institute for Worship Studies at (630) 510-8905.

INTRODUCTION

Enter His Courts with Praise: A Study of the Role of Music and the Arts in Worship may be used for personal study or a small-group course of study and spiritual formation. It is designed around thirteen easy-to-understand sessions. Each session has a two-part study guide. The first part is an individual study that each person completes privately. The second part is a one-hour interaction and application session that group members complete together (during the week or in an adult Sunday school setting). The first part helps you recall and reflect on what you've read, while the small-group study applies the material to each member's personal life and experience of public worship.

Enter His Courts with Praise is designed for use by one or more people. When the course is used in a group setting, the person who is designated as the leader simply needs to lead the group through the lesson step by step. It is always best to choose a leader before you begin.

Here are some suggestions for making your group discussions lively and insightful.

SUGGESTIONS FOR THE STUDENT

A few simple guidelines will help you use the study guide most effectively. They can be summarized under three headings: Prepare, Participate, and Apply.

Prepare

1. Answer each question in the study guide, "Part I: Personal Study," thoughtfully and critically.

2. Do all your work prayerfully. Prayer itself is worship. As you increase your knowledge of worship, do so in a spirit of prayerful openness before God.

Participate

1. Don't be afraid to ask questions. Your questions may give voice to the other members in the group. Your courage in speaking out will give others permission to talk and may encourage more stimulating discussion.

2. Don't hesitate to share your personal experiences. Abstract thinking has its place, but personal illustrations will help you and others remember the material more vividly.

3. Be open to others. Listen to the stories that other members tell, and respond to them in a way that does not invalidate their experiences.

Apply

1. Always ask yourself, "How can this apply to worship?"

2. Commit yourself to being a more intentional worshiper. Involve yourself in what is happening around you.

3. Determine your gifts. Ask yourself, "What can I do in worship that will minister to the body of Christ?" Then offer your gifts and talents to worship.

SUGGESTIONS FOR THE LEADER

Like the worship that it advocates, the group study in *Enter His Courts with Praise* is dialogic in nature. Because this study has been developed around the principles of discussion and sharing, a monologue or lecture approach will not work. The following guidelines will help you encourage discussion, facilitate learning, and implement the practice of worship. Use these guidelines with "Part II: Group Discussion" in each session.

1. Encourage the participants to prepare thoroughly and to bring their Bibles and study guides to each session.

2. Begin each session with prayer. Since worship is a kind of prayer, learning about worship should be a prayerful experience.

3. Discuss each question individually. Ask for several answers and encourage people to react to comments made by others.

4. Use a chalkboard or flip chart or dry-erase board. Draw charts and symbols that visually enhance the ideas being presented. Outline major concepts.

5. Look for practical applications of answers and suggestions that are offered. Try asking questions like, "How would you include this in our worship?" "How would you feel about that change?" "How does this insight help you to be a better worshiper?"

6. Invite concrete personal illustrations. Ask questions like, "Have you experienced that? Where? When? Describe how you felt in that particular situation."

7. When you have concluded Session 9, send the names and addresses of all the students who will complete the class to: Institute for Worship Studies, Box 894, Wheaton, IL 60189. We will then send a certificate of accomplishment for each student in time for you to distribute them during the last class. The cost of each certificate is $1.00. (Add $3.00 for postage and handling.)

One final suggestion: Purchase the larger work upon which this course is based, volume 4 of *The Complete Library of Christian Worship*. This volume, entitled *Music and the Arts in Christian Worship*, comprises a pair of beautiful 8½-by-11-inch coffee table books—the first concentrating on music and the second on the other arts—that will inform your mind and inspire your heart through hours of reading and study.

MUSIC AND THE ARTS IN BIBLICAL WORSHIP

A Study in Encounter with God through the Arts

 My contact with music and the arts in worship goes all the way back to my preschool days in Africa. My parents were missionaries in the small village of Mitulu in what was known at the time as the Belgian Congo.

Music and the arts have always been central to African culture. As the Africans were evangelized, they brought their instruments, their music, and their arts into the worship of the church. I can still remember the beat of the drums, the lyrical chants, and the ring dances that characterized African music.

My most memorable experience of music and the arts in worship came from the annual Easter pageant at Mitulu. The village was situated at the foot of a small mountain of sculptured rock called Mount Beli. It was beautiful, with shrubs, plants, and flowers growing from its many crags. Early on Easter Sunday morning, the villagers all assembled at the foot of the mountain and climbed to the top, where they gathered flowers. With flowers in hand, they marched down the mountain single file singing songs of the resurrection. Their worship march ended at our home, where they planted new flowers and concluded their sunrise service.

In this experience and in all the worship experiences of the church, music and the arts not only communicate the joy of coming together to enact God's saving deed in Christ, but also communicate the message. The "medium," as Marshall McLuhan said, "is the message." This contemporary axiom also holds true for biblical times.

MUSIC IN OLD TESTAMENT TIMES

A study of music in the Old Testament demonstrates that there were two traditions of music in the worship of Israel. The first was informal, spontaneous, and ecstatic. The second was formal and professional.

The more informal approach to music in worship is demonstrated when the prophet Samuel speaks to Saul of an encounter that he will have with a group of prophets engaging in a spontaneous form of worship. Samuel says that the prophets will be "coming down from the high place with lyres, tambourines, flutes and harps . . . and they will be prophesying." For Saul, the result of this free-flowing worship and music service will be that the "Spirit of the LORD will come upon you in power, and you will prophesy with them; and you will be changed into a different person" (1 Sam 10:5–6).

This free-flowing service is very similar to the kind of spontaneous worship and music that characterize contemporary charismatic or praise and worship traditions of worship.

A second form of worship and music in the Old Testament is the more formal tradition associated with temple worship. This musical tradition was established by King David who was, as we all know, a highly talented musician and composer of hymns. David instructed the leaders of the Levites to appoint singers of joyful songs accompanied by the sounds of musical instruments such as lyres, harps, and cymbals (1 Chron 15:16).

In temple worship the congregation did not sing. Its role was to listen and respond with an amen, an alleluia, or possibly an antiphon, especially with the psalms. This second form of music in worship is similar to traditional worship today.

MUSIC IN NEW TESTAMENT TIMES

The New Testament is full of the songs of the early church, such as the Magnificat (Luke 1:46–55), the Benedictus (Luke 1:68–79), the Gloria in Excelsis Deo (Luke 2:14), and the Nunc Dimittis (Luke 2:29–32). These canticles have been sung throughout the history of the church in traditional worship. Our thoughts also turn to the songs in the book of Revelation, songs that the composer Handel included in his renowned *Messiah*, which is sung around the world every Christmas.

Most of us associate New Testament music with Paul's admonition to sing "psalms, hymns and spiritual songs" (Eph 5:19). Let's look at these three types of music.

- ◆ Psalms. The New Testament church continued many of the traditions of synagogue worship, including a strong emphasis on psalm singing. The book of Psalms was the songbook of the early church.
- ◆ Hymns. The hymns of the early church were a new expression of singing. Scholarship has been able to identify some of these hymns in the New

Testament text; they are called "Christ hymns." The most famous of these hymns include Philippians 2:6–11, John 1:1–14, and Colossians 1:15–20. Other important hymns include 1 Timothy 3:16 and 2 Timothy 2:11–13.

- ◆ Spiritual songs. The Greek phrase for spiritual songs may be translated "pneumatic odes." The reference here is to breath or spirit as in spontaneous or ecstatic forms of song. We do know that the early church sang a melismatic and prolonged final syllable of the "alleluias." Augustine describes this kind of singing as "a certain sound of joy without words . . . it is the expression of the mind poured forth in joy" (Nicene and Post-Nicene Fathers, 1.8.488). This kind of singing, historically called jubilus, may correspond to the more ecstatic expressions detailed by Paul in 1 Corinthians 12–14.

Today in worship renewal—both traditional and contemporary—these three forms of music are finding their way into worship. Traditional churches have always sung the hymns of the church. Contemporary churches have rediscovered the more ecstatic forms of worship, and new forms of music for the psalms have emerged in both traditional and contemporary churches.

The Arts in Old Testament Worship

Whenever the arts are mentioned in reference to worship, the Second Commandment and its prohibition against making a graven image of God comes up. Unfortunately, many Protestants have interpreted this command as prohibiting any kind of artistic symbolism. Protestant churches consequently tend to shun visual art.

Apparently the Old Testament believers did not hold to such a severe interpretation of the commandment. They did not adorn the temple with representations of God, but they did beautify the temple with all kinds of art and symbolism. (See the elaborate and artistic instructions for building the tabernacle in Exodus 25:10–22.)

It is important to remember that the art and symbolism of the temple was never meant as "art for art's sake." It was not on display. The temple was a place to encounter God, not a museum. The art in the temple was a vehicle by which an encounter was to take place. The arts "spoke," as it were. Art communicated truth about God. Art communicated the beauty, the sovereignty, the holiness of God. Worshipers met the God of beauty and holiness through the truth spoken by the art and symbolism of the temple.

THE ARTS IN NEW TESTAMENT WORSHIP

A very significant change in the use of art in worship occurred in the New Testament era. God had become incarnate and was now actually imaged in the person of Jesus (Col 1:15). In the incarnation the unimaginable had become human. God had become an actual living human being. God could be seen, heard, spoken to, and touched (1 John 1:1). Here was the glory of God enfleshed (John 1:14).

Recognizing God's presence in Jesus, the early church continued to retain the symbols God had ordained to be the links between the divine and the human. Symbolic forms of communication such as parables and stories were collected in books. Through these stories the community experienced the very presence of Jesus. An encounter with Jesus occurred through the visible and tangible signs of bread, wine, oil, and the water of baptism. These symbols and signs have always been at the very heart of Christian worship and remain today as a primary means of an encounter with God.

Throughout history many of the churches have held to the principle that art is a vehicle through which God continues to speak. The Orthodox Church has expressed God's presence in icons, the Catholic Church through great cathedrals, art objects, and stained glass. While Protestants have been more restrained in their use of the arts, many churches have given careful attention to architecture and to the beauty of the pulpit, the Communion table, and the baptismal font or pool. The arts are still alive in contemporary worship and are finding a new place in the worship of both traditional and contemporary churches.

CONCLUSION

This brief introduction has shown that music and the arts played an important role in biblical worship. They were a voice through which God communicated. Today God's people are anxious to hear from God. The authoritative voice of God is heard primarily in Scripture. But the message of God may be communicated to us in nonverbal ways as well. It may be reflected in music and the arts. Surely the Scriptures present music and the arts as poetic and majestic ways to encounter the living Word in worship!

STUDY GUIDE

Read Session 1, "Music and the Arts in Biblical Worship,"
before answering these questions.

PART I: PERSONAL STUDY

Answer the following questions on your own.

1. *Life Connection*

◆ We have seen how significant music and the arts are as a form of communication. Recount an instance in your life in which you sensed how Christian music or Christian art actually communicated to your spirit.

_____

_____

_____

2. *Content Questions*

◆ Explain how informal music ministered to Saul. (See 1 Samuel 10:5-6.)

_____

_____

_____

◆ A more formal use of music is described in 1 Chronicles 15:16, 19–22. Read this passage and describe what you think your emotions would have been in that service. _____

_____

_____

◆ Look up one (or more) of the biblical sources of the great canticles of the church. Jot down your emotional response to the canticle.

The Magnificat (my soul magnifies) of Mary (Luke 1:46–55) _____

_____

The Benedictus (blessed be God) of Zechariah (Luke 1:68–79) _____

_____

The Gloria in Excelsis Deo (glory to God in the highest) of the angels
(Luke 2:14) _____

_____

_____

The Nunc Dimittis (now you let your servant depart in peace) of Simeon
(Luke 2:29–32) _____

_____

_____

◆ In your own words, describe the following types of song sung in the early
  church.
  Psalms _____

_____

  Hymns _____

_____

  Spiritual songs _____

_____

◆ For your own edification and spiritual enjoyment read (or sing) each of
  the following "Christ hymns" of the early church. Describe your emotional response to each hymn.
  Philippians 2:6–11 _____

_____

  John 1:1–14 _____

_____

  Colossians 1:15–20 _____

_____

  1 Timothy 3:16 _____

_____

  2 Timothy 2:11–13 _____

_____

_____

◆ To appreciate more deeply the place of the arts in worship, read Exodus 25:10–22. Can you find a statement in this passage that suggests the purpose of this artistically appointed setting? Jot it down below.

_____

_____

_____

_____

◆ Explain how the incarnation can be described as the glory of God manifest. You may want to look up Colossians 1:15 and John 1:14.

_____

_____

_____

_____

◆ Explain how the following may be described as art through which God is encountered:

Parables _____

_____

Stories _____

_____

Bread and wine _____

_____

Water _____

_____

Oil _____

_____

3. *Application*

◆ Think about a recent service of worship in your church. How much of what you have studied in this session did you actually experience in that service? _____

_____

_____

_____

PART II: GROUP DISCUSSION

Share the insights you gained from your personal study in Part I. Write out all answers that group members give to the questions on a chalkboard, a flip chart, or a dry erase board.

1. *Life Connection*

◆ Begin by having several members of the group share the experience of music or the arts in which they felt an encounter or engagement with God.

2. *Thought Questions*

◆ Today many churches seem to be divided over using informal or formal music in worship. Imagine that Saul and David were featured on a contemporary TV talk show discussing music in the church. What would they say to us? If you want to be creative and have some fun with this question, find Saul and David impersonators in the class and conduct a talk show program with interaction from the audience.

◆ If you have time, sing one of the great canticles of the church: the Magnificat, the Benedictus, the Gloria in Excelsis Deo, or the Nunc Dimittis. Or obtain a recording of a musical setting of one or more of these canticles and listen to it (your local Christian bookstore can order one for you). After you have sung or listened to one of the canticles, spend some time thinking about the kind of response toward God that this music elicited from your mind, your heart, and your will. You may want to write out these thoughts.

◆ Now sing one of the Christ hymns of the early church (Phil 2:6–11; John 1:1–14; Col 1:15–20; 1 Tim 3:16; 2 Tim 2:11–13). We don't know how these texts were sung, so you can have a member of your group improvise. To encourage participation, use the form of singing known as "lining out": the leader sings a phrase, the group responds, and so on, until the entire text has been sung. What kind of response toward God did this song elicit from your mind, your heart, your will?

- Now sing a psalm, a hymn, and a spiritual song. How did each of these types of song speak to your heart?

- Ask members of the group to tell about the most artistically appointed church they have seen. How did the artistic environment of this church elicit a response toward God from them?

- Ask the members of the group to explain how God may have encountered them in one or more of the following art form experiences:

  A parable used in a sermon

  A "storytelling" of the gospel lesson

  A spiritual encounter through the experience of bread and wine (describe the artistic form)

  A spiritual encounter through the experience of the water of baptism (describe the artistic form)

  A spiritual encounter through the anointing of oil (describe the artistic form)

3. Application

- Choose one or more of the following forms of music to incorporate into the worship of your church:

  More informal music

  More formal music

  More canticles

  More Christ hymns

  More psalms

  More hymns

  More spiritual songs

  Note: You may want to poll the class to gauge the general disposition of the congregation toward each form of music. Then ask, "How, when, and where would we make these changes?"

- Which of the following artistic means of communication would you like to experience more frequently in the worship of your church?

  Parables

  Gospel storytelling

  A more artistically formed experience of Communion

  A more artistically formed water baptism

  A more artistically formed anointing of oil with the laying on of hands

  ("Artistically formed" actions are done deliberately, in good form and with spiritual intention, as opposed to sloppily or without spiritual intention.)

- You may want to poll the group to gauge the general disposition of the congregation toward each form of communication. Then ask, "How, when, and where would we make these changes?"

- How may the study and application of this session help you improve the worship of your church?

PART I

MUSIC IN

WORSHIP

THE PURPOSE OF MUSIC IN WORSHIP

A Study in the Content and Meaning of Encounter

 The Episcopal Church is best known for the *Book of Common Prayer,* which goes all the way back to the time of the Reformation. Thomas Cranmer, the English reformer who shaped this book, drew on sources that went back to the medieval church and the early church. The book has gone through numerous revisions, but it endures as the centerpiece of Episcopal worship, theology, and piety.

Almost every Episcopal church has what is called the prayer book service. This service is usually conducted at 8 a.m. on Sunday. Some people simply call it the eight o'clock service. If you attended this service, you would discover that it goes through the prayer book in a simple and plain manner. The celebrant leads the congregation in the set prayers, the versicles, and the Scripture. It is a quiet, simple service. There is no organ, no singing, no music whatsoever. And yet it is a powerful service of worship.

The fact that worship can be accomplished without music raises the question, What is the purpose of music in worship?

THE PURPOSE OF MUSIC IN WORSHIP

In Session 1 we saw that music can enable an encounter with the living God. The word *encounter* is freighted with meaning. We encounter people, ideas, situations, and the like. We "bump up against" or "interact with" something "other." In the case of music in worship we are being encountered by God and God's truth.

An encounter with God generally has three aspects: (1) the content of the encounter, (2) the manner or mode whereby the content is proclaimed, and (3) our response to the encounter.

MUSIC AS CONTENT

The *content* of worship is the story of the meaning of human existence. In a church I attended some time ago, the worship leader led the congregation in a memorable prayer:

> Lord, we give you thanks that you created us in your image. When we fell away from you into sin, you did not leave us in our sin, but you came to us in Jesus Christ, who lived among us, died for us, was resurrected from the dead, ascended into heaven, is seated at the right hand of the Father and will come again to restore the world. Bless us as we worship in his name.

This prayer swept from creation to re-creation and expressed the litany of ideas that constitute the gospel message. Throughout history the music of the church has conveyed this context.

The Bible contains many songs that tell the story of God's marvelous works. The morning stars "sang together" at creation (Job 38:7). The people of Israel sang a song of deliverance from Egypt (Exod 15:1–18). The psalmist sings a song of marvelous praise because God "has done marvelous things" (Ps 98:1). The New Testament canticles, such as the Magnificat (Luke 1:46–55) and the Benedictus (Luke 1:68–79), are songs that celebrate the story of God's saving deeds in the birth of Christ. The concluding book of the Bible, the book of Revelation, is full of songs that tell the story of how God in Jesus Christ has overcome the power of the evil one.

In worship, our hymns, canticles, Scripture songs, gospel songs, and contemporary choruses deal with the story. Each song may not deal with the whole story of the Christian faith, but it deals with part of the story. Thus one major purpose of worship is, in the words of the song, to "tell me the old, old story." This is the content of the encounter.

MUSIC AS PROCLAMATION

The content of an encounter with God may be proclaimed through the reading of Scripture, through preaching, and in many other ways. Singing is one of the ways in which the content is proclaimed.

To say that music is sung proclamation is to say that music proclaims the gospel story. The word *proclaim* means "to herald, to tell out, to declare." Through music we preach and admonish. This is the meaning of Paul's teaching in Ephesians 5:18–19, where he instructs us to be filled with the Spirit, addressing one another in psalms, hymns, and spiritual songs. When we come together in worship, it is to proclaim and enact the gospel story and to be shaped by it as it takes up residence within us. The apostle Paul says that this can happen by singing!

Luther recognized the life-giving significance of song proclamation: "St. Paul . . . in his Epistle to the Colossians insists that Christians appear before God with Psalms and spiritual songs which emanate from the heart, in order that through these the word of God and Christian doctrine may be preached, taught, and put into practice" (preface to *Geistliche Gesangbuchlein*, 1524).

Singing continues to proclaim God's story and truth. Choir anthems, solos, hymns, canticles, and choruses often proclaim how God rescues us from our dislocated condition and relocates our lives in God.

MUSIC AS A PRAYER OF RESPONSE

The word "response" has two distinct meanings in the context of worship. First, the proclamation of God's story demands a *response*. It is not meant to fall on deaf ears or to be ignored. God's word is active and creative, and it creates a response within us—often in the form of a song. Response to God's proclamation and presence in worship has, from the very beginning of time, been expressed through sung prayer. Second, in the temple and in the synagogue, prayer was often expressed through a sung verse followed by a response. We refer to this practice as responsive reading, recitation, or singing; i.e., the people *respond* to a worship leader, or different parts of the congregation *respond* to each other. This practice continues in liturgical churches today. Here is an example:

Verse:	May God be gracious to us and bless us
Response:	And make his face shine upon us;
Verse:	May your ways be known on earth
Response:	Your salvation among all nations.
Verse:	May the people praise you, O God;
Response:	May all the peoples praise you. (Ps 67:1–3)

The book of Psalms, which was sung in worship, contains many prayers that are responsive in both senses of the word. Psalm 80 was sung responsively in the synagogue and later in the church.

Hear us, O Shepherd of Israel,
   you who lead Joseph like a flock;
you who sit enthroned between the cherubim, shine forth
   before Ephraim, Benjamin and Manasseh.

Awaken your might;
  come and save us.

Restore us, O God;
  make your face shine upon us,
  that we may be saved. (Ps 80:1–3)

Jonah prayed from the belly of the whale. Jonah's prayer, which is a cry for help, is recorded in Jonah 2. The prayer begins, "In my distress I called to the LORD, and he answered me" (2:2), and it ends, "But I, with a song of thanksgiving, will sacrifice to you" (2:9).

Sung responses to God's proclamation (usually taken from the Psalms) have been an essential part of worship from the earliest times. They occur after the reading from the Old Testament, the Epistle, or the Gospel. Sung responses expressing the faith of the church are often sung after the sermon. There are also sung responses in the eucharistic prayer, such as the Sanctus, "Holy, Holy, Holy." The songs people sing as they receive Communion are also sung prayers of response, in which people lift their hearts and voices to God.

CONCLUSION

We began by asking the question, What is the purpose of music in worship? I hope that you now have a good idea of how to answer that question. It's very simple. The content of worship, which is the biblical story, may be sung forth. This singing is a proclamation of truth, to which the people may respond in sung prayer.

Does music have a place in worship? Yes. Like *The Book of Common Prayer*, it tells the story. Only it sings it!

STUDY GUIDE

Read Session 2, "The Purpose of Music in Worship,"
before answering these questions.

PART I: PERSONAL STUDY

Answer the following questions on your own.

1. *Life Connection*

◆ In this session we addressed the purpose of music in worship. We began
with an illustration of worship without music. Describe a worship service
you participated in that had no music. Then describe one that had music.
Compare your emotional response to each experience.

_____

_____

_____

_____

_____

2. *Content Questions*

◆ List the three elements of an encounter with God.

a. _____

_____

b. _____

_____

c. _____

_____

◆ Using your own words, describe music as content.

_____

_____

_____

_____

_____

- Our study made the claim that the purpose of music is to tell the story (content). Read the songs in each of these Scripture texts and comment on the story that each one tells.
  Exodus 15:1–18 _____

  _____

  Luke 1:46–55 _____

  _____

  Revelation 4–5 _____

  _____

- Using your own words, describe what it means to say that music is a proc-lamation. _____

  _____

  _____

- The cry "Abba, Father" may have been a spiritual song in the early church. What does it proclaim? (See Romans 8:15–17.)

  _____

  _____

  _____

  _____

- Using your own words, describe what it means to say that music is a prayer of response. _____

  _____

  _____

  _____

- Historically, the church has sung Psalm 52 as a prayer of response, espe-cially during Lent. Read this passage, then outline and comment on it.

  _____

  _____

  _____

  _____

3. *Application*

◆ Think through a recent worship service. How did the music of that worship tell the story, proclaim God's story, and elicit a response in your heart?

PART II: GROUP DISCUSSION

Share the insights you gained from your personal study in Part I. Write out all answers that group members give to the questions on a chalkboard, a flip chart, or a dry erase board.

1. *Life Connection*

◆ Ask students to compare services in which there was (1) no music or (2) good music. See if members of the group have a common response to these two expressions of worship.

2. *Thought Questions*

◆ Discuss the story of Exodus 15:1–18. Allow everyone to share personal insights. Then sing the contemporary song, "The Horse and the Rider He Has Thrown into the Sea." Finally, ask the class to share their emotional response to the story of the song. How did they encounter God and God's truth?

◆ Discuss the proclamation content of Philippians 2:5–11. Ask group members to contribute their insights on this passage. Then sing "Crown Him with Many Crowns" followed by "He Is Lord." Finally, ask the members to share their emotional response to what these songs proclaim.

◆ Discuss the content of Psalm 52. Ask the group members to share their experience of working with this passage. Then improvise a tune and sing the psalm lined out; i.e., the leader sings one line at a time, with the group repeating each line. Follow the singing of the psalm with the contemporary song, "Create in Me a Clean Heart, O God." Finally discuss the encounter experienced in these songs.

♦ If you have time, walk through the repertoire of hymns and choruses you generally use in your church and identify songs of content (story), proclamation, and response. Sing some of the songs. Discuss your experience of how music is an encounter with God and God's truth.

3. *Application*

♦ Analyze how the music in a recent worship service accomplished its purpose—an encounter with God through God's content proclaimed and received with heartfelt response.

♦ Plan the music for an upcoming service and carefully include story, proclamation, and response.

♦ How has this study helped you appreciate the ministry of music in worship?

THE PLACE OF PRAISE MUSIC IN WORSHIP

A Study in Expressing Our Relationship to God

 I grew up in a traditional church and have always worshiped in churches that are hymn-driven rather than chorus-driven. For that reason I was rather skeptical of the chorus movement when it emerged in the 1960s.

My first experience of a chorus-oriented church occurred in the early 1970s when I visited a Pentecostal church. Many Pentecostal churches combine hymns and choruses, but this particular church did not. It was a chorus-driven church.

I don't remember everything about that occasion, but I do remember that we began by singing, "There's a sweet, sweet spirit in this place, and I know it's the spirit of the Lord." The chorus was sung in an intentional and moving way. My experience with the people of that church turned out to be consistent with the song. They were open, inviting people who were characterized by the spiritual hospitality of the song.

Praise choruses have won a place in many traditional churches. In this session we will address the place of praise choruses in worship. We want to ask, Why sing a praise chorus?

THE BIBLICAL MANDATE OF PRAISE

The Scriptures say a great deal about praise. According to the psalms, the entire creation was made to praise God. Many psalms call on the sun, the moon, the stars, and all creatures small and great to praise the Lord. Two favorite praise psalms are Psalm 96 and Psalm 150. The psalmist writes "Sing to the LORD a new song, sing to the LORD all the earth" (96:1). Psalm 150 ends with the words, "Let everything that has breath praise the LORD."

Praise lies at the very center of the created order and at the very heart of human existence. The whole created order and all its beings are to be ablaze with praise. The angels praise God: "Praise him, all his angels, praise him, all his heavenly hosts" (Ps 148:2). Isaiah had a vision of heavenly worship and heard the seraphs sing, "Holy, Holy, Holy is the LORD Almighty; the whole earth is full of his glory" (Isa 6:3). John saw into the heavens and there around the throne of God heard the heavenly hosts forever praising God (Rev 4:8–11; 5:6–14). Isaiah captures this cosmic experience of praise when he cries

Sing for joy, O heavens, . . .
    shout aloud, O earth beneath.
Burst into song, you mountains,
    you forests and all your trees. (Isa 44:23)

The psalmist similarly instructs God's people to break forth in song:

Sing for joy to God our strength;
    shout aloud to the God of Jacob!
Begin the music, strike the tambourine,
    play the melodious harp and lyre. (Ps 81:1–2)

These scriptural admonitions to give praise to God could be repeated a thousand times. There can be no question that praise has an indispensable place in our worship!

WHAT DOES PRAISE DO?

Why praise God? Do we praise God simply because we are told to do so, or are there some benefits to praise?

First, praise is always associated with the presence of God. God, the Scriptures declare, is enthroned on the praises of God's people (Ps 22:3 [NIV mg., RSV]; 100:4). This is interpreted to mean that our worship enthrones God. Because it does so, it puts us in our rightful place: on our knees worshiping the Almighty! We recognize God as the Creator and the sovereign Lord, and ourselves as creatures of the Almighty.

Second, praise testifies. It declares and proclaims God's mighty deeds. It acknowledges what God has done. This facet of praise is akin to the way praise works in our own lives. We like to praise people who have done well, and we like to be praised. I have tried to follow this rule in my own life. When my children have done well, succeeding in school or sports or work, I want to acknowledge and praise them for what they have done. When we praise our children or spouse or co-workers, we testify to their worth and value. So it is with God. Peter tells us: "you are a chosen people, a royal priesthood, a holy nation, a people belonging to God, that you may declare the praises of him who called you out of darkness into his wonderful light" (1 Pet 2:9). In worship we praise and acknowledge God for God's wonderful saving deeds.

Third, praise has the power to deliver us. All of us wrestle with something—depression, sadness, loneliness, fear, insecurity, sickness, pain. Praise does not necessarily put these problems to rest, but praise brings comfort and solace in the midst of these trials. Praise is a way of putting all these matters into perspective. Isaiah speaks to the delivering power of praise in these words:

> The Spirit of the sovereign LORD is on me . . .
> to comfort all who mourn,
>   and provide for those who grieve in Zion—
> to bestow on them a crown of beauty
>   instead of ashes,
> the oil of gladness
>   instead of mourning,
> and a garment of praise
>   instead of a spirit of despair. (Isa 61:1–3)

We don't praise God in order to obtain these benefits. Praise is not a way to manipulate God to get what we want or to gain special favors. No! True praise arises out of a thankful and grateful heart. Our praise has to be characterized by integrity and a spirit of genuine appreciation. It is this kind of praise that God wants and honors.

WHERE DOES PRAISE FIT INTO WORSHIP?

Worship is modeled on a fourfold pattern: we gather, we hear God's word, we give thanks, and we are sent forth to love and serve God. We can visualize this pattern as follows:

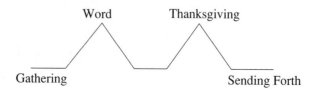

The gathering brings us into the presence of God and readies us to hear the word of the Lord. Songs of praise are appropriate at several points. Choruses may be used as people find their seats and prepare themselves for worship. In contemporary churches, choruses provide a thirty-minute approach to God. They follow the tabernacle model of entering progressively the gates, the outer court, the inner court, and finally the holy of holies. The content and mood of these choruses shift from exuberant praise to quiet meditative praise as the people of God enter, as it were, the holy of holies.

As the diagram indicates, the word spoken and the word enacted are the two high points of worship. The service of the word is primarily a time not for singing but for instruction in truth and holy living. Consequently, a chorus may be used in response to a Scripture reading or some other act of worship. For example, at the end of the Scripture reading the reader may declare, "This is the word of the Lord." The people could then sing "Thy Word Is a Lamp unto My Feet" or some other appropriate chorus. In traditional churches a psalm is sung after the reading. Many psalms have been put into the chorus genre; one of these may be used after any one of the Scripture readings as a response to God's word.

In many churches, the time between the service of the word and the service of thanksgiving is used for announcements and introduction of visitors. The worship through the word has ended. Now worship momentarily stops; then after the announcements worship begins again around the table.

Renewing churches express their thanksgiving in two ways: in Communion or, when Communion is not celebrated, in songs and prayers. Liturgical churches celebrate Communion weekly, but most other churches celebrate Communion on the first Sunday of the month. The congregation may sing choruses in unison as people come forward to receive the bread and the wine. These choruses may follow a sequence that remembers Christ's death, resurrection, and exaltation. In this way the people experience through music what Communion intends to do—enact the dying, rising, and exaltation of Jesus with thanksgiving for the salvation and healing that come to us through God's saving acts. The right blend of choruses sung at Communion has a powerful and moving effect on the spiritual experience of giving thanks.

In churches that do not celebrate the Lord's Table weekly, the congregation may spend some time in simply giving thanks with prayers and songs after the service of the word has ended. The selection of choruses may be organized around the Trinity—offering praise to God for who God is, offering praise to the Son for what the Son has done, offering praise to the Holy Spirit, invoking the presence of the Holy Spirit in the midst of the assembly.

Finally, the dismissal is the time to sing a song of going forth. A chorus that expresses the church's going forth into the world to love and serve the Lord may be appropriate, but generally the congregation sings a hymn at the dismissal.

CONCLUSION

Praise, as we have seen, is an important and indispensable element of our worship. Scripture testifies that all creation praises God. Scripture is clear that God is enthroned and glorified in our praise and that praise is a testimony to God's great saving deeds. Praise is also a means to deliver us from those aspects of life that may drain us and bring us to depression. The contemporary chorus movement has played an important role in recovering the element of praise, and it has gifted the church with many new songs that can help us fulfill our role as the people of praise.

STUDY GUIDE

Read Session 3, "The Place of Praise Music in Worship,"
before answering these questions.

PART I: PERSONAL STUDY

Answer the following questions on your own.

1. *Life Connection*

◆ Have you ever experienced a contemporary praise and worship service? If
so, recall that service below and comment on your response to it, especially to the choruses that are now known as praise songs. _____

_____

_____

_____

_____

2. *Content Questions*

◆ Take time to read and then sing the two psalms cited below. Record how
the words and the sound that you gave to them (either audibly or in your
imagination) formed within you a spirit of praise.
Psalm 96_____

_____

_____

_____

Psalm 150_____

_____

_____

_____

◆ Read Isaiah 6:1–8. Sing the song of the seraphs (verse 3). What words
would you use to describe the experience of Isaiah? _____

_____

_____

_____

- Read Revelation 4:1–11. Sing it. Then write a description of your own experience of praise. _____

  _____

  _____

  _____

  _____

  _____

- The Scriptures teach that God dwells in the praises of God's people. How is God's name is taught through the following Scriptures?

  Psalm 22:3 _____

  _____

  Psalm 100:4 _____

  _____

- Explain what it means to say that praise "testifies." _____

  _____

  _____

- Explain what it means to say that praise "has the power to deliver us."

  _____

  _____

  _____

- Explain how praise fits into the four parts of worship:
  Praise in the gathering _____

  _____

  Praise in the service of the word _____

  _____

  Praise in the service of thanksgiving_____

  _____

  Praise in the dismissal _____

  _____

3. *Application*

◆ How has this study improved or expanded your understanding of praise?

_____

_____

_____

_____

_____

PART II: GROUP DISCUSSION

Share the insights you gained from your personal study in Part I. Write out all answers that group members give to the questions on a chalkboard, a flip chart, or a dry erase board.

1. *Life Connection*

◆ Ask various group members to share their experiences in praise and worship services. Be prepared to hear responses ranging from very negative to highly positive.

2. *Thought Questions*

◆ Walk through the praise character of Psalm 96 and Psalm 150. Ask group members to share their experiences of studying, singing, and meditating on these two psalms. Sing one of them (line it out). Then ask, How does offering praise to God help establish your relationship with God?

◆ Ask group members to share their experiences of studying, singing, and reflecting on Isaiah 6:1–8. Sing "Holy, Holy, Holy, Lord God Almighty" and other versions of the Sanctus that you know. Ask, What do you experience when you sing the Sanctus?

◆ Read the following Scripture songs and discuss how they accomplish what is said of each.
Psalm 22:3: God dwells in the praises of God's people
Revelation 11:15–18: Praise testifies
Acts 16:16–34: Praise delivers

3. *Application*

+ Evaluate a recent service of your church and determine how praise to God was expressed throughout the service.

+ Act as a worship planning committee and develop a service of worship that clearly expresses praise to God in music (plan according to the four-fold pattern).

+ How has this study enriched your understanding and experience of praise to God through music?

PSALMS, HYMNS, AND SPIRITUAL SONGS

A Study in the Enthronement of God

 I have an observation that I want to present. It comes from my own experience, and I want you to test it by your own experience in the church.

I travel from church to church and from one Christian fellowship to another. My experience in worship ranges from high liturgical churches to some very freewheeling groups. What I have observed is this: most Christian denominations and groups have their own set of songs and generally do not borrow songs from other groups.

The Eastern Orthodox tradition has the Troparion and the Kontakion, which you simply don't find elsewhere. Catholic churches use a whole genre of music that most Protestants have never heard. Protestant churches have a common pool of hymnody, but if you study the new hymnbooks of the Episcopal, Lutheran, Methodist, Mennonite, and Presbyterian churches, you will find certain hymns and songs and styles of singing in each. For example, Mennonites use an unusually beautiful four-part unaccompanied harmony that is seldom heard elsewhere.

Newer churches are also contributing to this variety of hymnody and sounds: gospel, the singing in the spirit of Pentecostal and charismatic churches, and the chorus movement that has spread around the world. And then there is the particular sound and hymnody of African, African-American, Hispanic, Asian, and Caribbean peoples.

I think I have made my point. There are more songs and musical styles out there than any one church can use, and each church is somewhat limited in its choice of music.

I like to think that the eclectic use of music in worship is what Paul had in mind when he admonished the church: "Speak to one another with psalms, hymns, and spiritual songs" (Eph 5:19). In this session we'll look at these three kinds of singing and consider how they may be used in the worship of our church.

PSALMS

The theology of the psalms is complex, and space does not permit us to deal with that subject here. Nevertheless, allow me to make one theological statement that will frame our understanding of psalm singing.

The psalms are acts of praise. Many of the psalms were originally written for specific events in the life of Israel. Enthronement psalms, for example, were written to celebrate the yearly festival of enthroning the king as ruler over all of Israel. While a particular enthronement song may have been written for a specific historical occasion, its spiritual meaning pointed beyond the enthronement of the king to the enthronement of Christ. Psalm 110 says, "The LORD says to my Lord: 'Sit at my right hand'" (110:1). That verse in its cultural setting referred to the enthronement of the king of Israel. But its spiritual meaning refers to the enthronement of Jesus Christ. The writer of Hebrews quotes Psalm 110:1 in referring to Christ as the one who "sat down at the right hand of the Majesty in heaven" (see Heb 1:1–4).

When we sing a psalm we are, through our praise, actually acknowledging and enthroning God. Our worship puts God on the throne. It recognizes God as the ruler of the universe. It says, "God is King and I submit to God's rule in my life and over the whole world."

Now let's look at ways to sing those psalms that declare God's place in the universe.

- Metrical psalms. The Reformed and Presbyterian churches have handed down a style of singing the psalms that is quite energetic and moving. A metrical psalm is a psalm paraphrased into stanzas and sung to a well-known hymn tune.

- Chant psalms. Chanted psalms go all the way back to the early church. Chant is a popular form of singing that is a bit more complicated than the metrical psalm. Chant psalms are sung in unison by the entire congregation. The sound is normally meditative, the chant uses only a short range of notes.

- Responsorial psalms. When the congregation sings in a responsorial manner, the choir or the cantor sings the verse and the people respond with a refrain. Many responsorial psalms are included in new denominational hymn books.

- Chorus psalms. Contemporary music has also restored the psalms to worship. Contemporary musicians take a verse or a phrase from a psalm (seldom an entire psalm) and set it to a contemporary sound.

The place of psalm singing in worship is an important matter to consider as well. From the beginning of the church era, psalms have been sung after the reading of Scripture. They are a response to the proclamation of the word.

HYMNS

The word *hymn* comes from the Greek *hymnos*, which is interpreted as a song of praise to God. Though hymns were sung to pagan gods prior to the Christian era, Christians quickly adopted this form of song and addressed their songs to the triune God of the Bible.

The earliest hymns of the church were addressed to Christ as God (see Phil 2:5–11). Another early and very famous hymn of the church that is still sung today is the Gloria in Excelsis Deo. Some of the most familiar hymns of the church were written during its first thousand years: "Of the Father's Love Begotten" (A.D. 350); "Hail Thee, Festival Day" (A.D. 550); "All Glory, Laud, and Honor" (A.D. 760); "Come Holy Spirit, Our Souls Inspire" (A.D. 856); "O Sacred Head, Now Wounded" (A.D. 450) and "Jesus, the Very Thought of Thee" (A.D. 1150). These hymns are still found in nearly every hymnal.

The Reformation era also produced numerous hymn texts and tunes. Martin Luther put his finger on the importance of the hymn in these words:

> I have always loved music; whoso has skill in this art, is of a good temperament, fitted for all things. We much teach music in schools; a schoolmaster ought to have skill in music or I should reject him; neither shall we ordain young man as preachers unless they have been well exercised in music. (William Hazlitt, ed., *The Table Talk of Martin Luther* [United Lutheran Publishing House], 416)

In recent years the hymnbook and the more solid hymnody of the church have been in decline as the chorus movement has gained ascendancy in many places. But hymns should not be lost; they are vital to a healthy worship life. Hymns speak to the substance side of worship. They are directed toward God and teach truths about God's person and saving activity in history. Think of the doctrinal and educational element of the great hymns of the church, such as "The God of Abraham Praise" or "Immortal, Invisible, God Only Wise" or Luther's great hymn, "A Mighty Fortress Is Our God," or the great hymn of Charles Wesley, "O for a Thousand Tongues to Sing My Great Redeemer's Praise." These are treasures of the church that convey a message. They tell the story of God, proclaim the content of the Christian faith, and teach truth.

In worship, hymns may be used as processionals and recessionals and in response to Scripture and to sermons. Communion hymns move the heart in adoration and worship of God.

SPIRITUAL SONGS

Spiritual songs are less familiar than psalms or hymns. But spiritual songs are experiencing a significant comeback in worship today. They can be traced all the way back to the early church.

In the early church spiritual songs were called Jubilation (or *jubilus*). The word comes from the Latin *jubilatio*, which means "loud shouting, whooping." The term referred to the sound made by a farmer or a shepherd calling out to someone or rounding up animals. These sounds were wordless phrases much like the familiar yodel.

Jubilation was carried from the field into the worship of the early church. It was the custom of the congregation to sing an alleluia before the reading of the Gospel. The last *a* of *alleluia* was usually extended into a long, spontaneous, wordless song.

This kind of spontaneous outward expression of an inner spiritual experience has been recovered by the charismatic movement today. It is generally called "singing in the Spirit." The worship leader may begin with a set of songs that lead the congregation into an intense sense of God's presence. The singing is quiet, meditative, and intensely personal. In the stillness of that moment the worship leader may say "sing your own song to the Lord." The leader may quietly play the strings of the guitar as people, raising their voices in adoration of God, may sing a continuous note, fashion a phrase or a word, or simply utter a spontaneous sound. These sounds, gathered together in unison, raise a wordless sound of praise to God until the leader closes in prayer.

CONCLUSION

Our brief study has shown us that we can praise God through many and varied musical songs and sounds. We have touched on the three broad types of song mentioned by the apostle Paul. I hope this study stimulates you to expand your range of musical content and style and to discover the power that other traditions of music have to empower your worship.

┌───┐

STUDY GUIDE

Read Session 4, "Psalms, Hymns, and Spiritual Songs,"
before answering these questions.

PART I: PERSONAL STUDY

Answer the following questions on your own.

1. Life Application

◆ Each Christian group seems to have its own collection of music, which is
   heard within that fellowship or denomination, and seldom elsewhere.
   There is a common group of hymns and songs, such as "Amazing Grace" or
   "Holy, Holy, Holy," that is generally known by all. Try to determine whether
   the assertion that different groups have different hymnody is correct. Find
   out how many different traditions are represented in the class. Let each tradition introduce hymns, songs, and choruses that are peculiar to it.

2. Content Questions

◆ Explain in your own words what a psalm does. _____
   _____
   _____
   _____

◆ The text suggests that many psalms were originally written for specific
   historical occasions of festal worship in Israel. Below are several psalms
   with their specific historical setting. Read several of these psalms to grasp
   the idea of the psalm's reflecting a particular setting.

   Psalm 65: a psalm of thanksgiving for a bountiful harvest
   Psalm 84: a psalm extolling Zion as the sanctuary of God; possibly used
       by pilgrims making a trip to an annual festival of Israel
   Psalm 72: a psalm written for the king's accession to the throne; perhaps
       used on the day of Solomon's enthronement as king of Israel
   Psalm 24: a psalm written for the procession of the ark to Zion

└───┘

- Read the above psalms again and look for the spiritual meaning they have beyond the historical occasion for which they were written. How may the psalm refer to Christ, to the church, or to our worship today?

Psalm 65 _____

_____

Psalm 84 _____

_____

Psalm 72 _____

_____

Psalm 24 _____

_____

- In your own words describe what it means to say that a psalm enthrones God. _____

_____

_____

_____

_____

- Describe the method of singing each kind of psalm:

Metrical psalms _____

_____

Chant psalms _____

_____

Responsorial psalms_____

_____

Chorus psalms _____

_____

- What is the origin and meaning of the word *hymn?*_____

_____

_____

_____

_____

- Borrow a hymnbook and read or sing to yourself one of the following ancient and medieval hymns:
  "Of the Father's Love Begotten" (A.D. 350)
  "Hail Thee, Festival Day" (A.D. 550)
  "Come Holy Spirit, Our Souls Inspire" (A.D. 856)
  "O Sacred Head, Now Wounded" (A.D. 1150)
  "Jesus, the Very Thought of Thee" (A.D. 1150)

- What do you think of Luther's statement on music? Do you agree?

  _____

  _____

  _____

- Using your hymnbook, study the content of one of the following hymns, then describe what truths about God the hymn teaches: "The God of Abraham Praise";"Immortal, Invisible, God Only Wise"; "A Mighty Fortress Is Our God"; "O for a Thousand Tongues to Sing."

  _____

  _____

  _____

  _____

- Describe the spiritual song of the early church called Jubilation.

  _____

  _____

  _____

- Use your own words to describe "singing in the Spirit." _____

  _____

  _____

  _____

3. Application

- As you have worked through these psalms, hymns, and spiritual songs, have you had a spiritual experience? Describe it. _____

  _____

  _____

PART II: GROUP DISCUSSION

Share the insights you gained from your personal study in Part I. Write out all answers that group members give to the questions on a chalkboard, a flip chart, or a dry erase board.

1. *Life Connection*

◆ Begin your discussion by asking members of the group from different traditions to identify the songs peculiar to their own tradition. What can we learn from each other?

2. *Thought Questions*

◆ Take time to read through one (or more) of the following psalms, interpreting it according to its historical setting; try to be elaborate as possible in your imaginative description of its original use. Then interpret the psalm according to its spiritual meaning, as praise to God that can be used by any group of people anywhere at any time.
Psalm 65, 84, 72, 24

_____

_____

_____

_____

◆ Discuss each of the following approaches to psalm singing:

Metrical singing
Chant singing
Responsorial singing
Chorus singing

◆ Now sing a psalm according to each method. For help consult your music minister, worship leader, or anyone in the church who is musically talented. You may also find some help in your hymnbook. If all else fails, improvise.

◆ Define spiritual songs. Do you think spiritual songs have a place in contemporary worship, or were they only for the New Testament church?

- Try singing according to the spiritual song genre or style.

  For example, sing the contemporary alleluia and at the leader's guidance allow the final *a* to move you into a free-flowing experience of sound without words.

- Sing a set of songs that leads you into a quiet, meditative relationship with God. End your singing with the chorus "I Love You, Lord." Allow this chorus to lead you into a time of communal singing during which each person offers words or songs of praise.

3. *Application*

- Evaluate your church's use of psalms, hymns, and spiritual songs over the last few months (you may want to look at some past bulletins). Is there one style of music you use over and over again? It there one style of music you neglect? Is your use of music balanced?

- Plan a worship service using the fourfold pattern of gathering, hearing the word, giving thanks, and sending forth. Where would you include hymns, psalms, and spiritual songs?

- How has this study helped you experience the enthronement of God through your praises?

Instruments in Worship

A Study in the Sound of Praise

 Because I grew up in Africa, I had no contact with traditional worship instruments until we returned to the United States. I was seven years old before I ever saw a church organ!

My parents were missionaries in a small jungle clearing. I was familiar with the sounds of the jungle, both around our house and in African instrumentation. But I was not familiar with the sounds of the organ or brass and wind instruments.

When we returned to the States, we lived in a missionary home in New Jersey called the "Houses of Fellowship" for a year while my parents figured out their next move in ministry. On that block was a very small and beautiful Anglican church. Although we were Baptist, we visited that church from time to time.

I always walked up to the front row and sat there by myself right under the pastor's nose. I don't remember much from those experiences except that I was drawn into the worship by the beauty of the church and the glorious sounds of the organ and the other instruments.

Instruments played an important role in the worship of biblical times and throughout the history of the church. In this session we are going to study the role of instruments in worship, as well as their propriety and use.

Instruments in Worship during Biblical Times

Instruments are referred to frequently in connection with the traditional worship of the Old Testament. Second Chronicles records how the ark was brought to the temple with the enormous sound of accompanying instrumentation:

> All the Levites who were musicians . . . stood on the east side of the altar, dressed in fine linen and playing cymbals, harps and lyres. They were accompanied by 120 priests sounding trumpets. The trumpeters and singers joined in unison, as with one voice, to give praise and thanks to the

LORD. Accompanied by trumpets, cymbals and other instruments, they raised their voices in praise to the LORD. (2 Chron 5:12–13)

The psalms contain numerous references to the use of instruments in worship. One of the most striking catalogs of instruments is found in Psalm 150:

Praise him with the sounding of the trumpet,
  praise him with the harp and lyre,
praise him with tambourine and dancing,
  praise him with the strings and flute,
praise him with the clash of cymbals. . . . (Ps 150: 3–5)

To Have or Not to Have

The use of instruments in worship has not always been accepted. Some churches today eschew instruments, most notably the Eastern Orthodox Church and Protestant bodies such as the Churches of Christ (noninstrumental), some Mennonite bodies, and some Presbyterians. The main historical sources of the objection to this use of instruments in worship were the early church fathers and the reformer John Calvin (although most Presbyterian and Reformed churches use instruments today). Three objections have been posited.

The first objection, voiced by the early church fathers, is that instruments were associated with pagan music and rituals. The early church was surrounded by a decadent culture that used instruments in pagan rituals, in the theater, in pagan banquets, in drunken carousing, and in immoral sexual rites. These instruments were so closely connected with paganism that to admit them into worship would have compromised the integrity of worship.

The second objection to the use of instruments in worship, which was made by both the early church fathers and John Calvin, is that worship is to be centered on the word. They argued that instruments interfered with the hearing of the pure word and should not be admitted to worship. In the fourth century Saint Basil urged worshipers, "While your tongue sings, let your mind search out the meaning of the words, so that you might sing in spirit and sing also in understanding" (James McKinnon, *Music in Early Christian Literature* [Cambridge University Press, 1987], p. 66).

The third objection to instrumentation in worship is that Christians are to sing with "one voice" (see Rom 15:5–6). The principle of "one voice" addresses the issue of community, or *koinōnia*. Instruments get in the way, it is charged, of unison singing. In unison singing the church confesses its one faith, its one heart, its one mind, its one Lord.

Obviously not all Christians reject instruments in worship. For many churches instrumentation in worship is not an issue. The theological argument in support of instrumentation in worship derives from the incarnation. God, it is argued, became one of us. God's incarnation in Jesus Christ sets up the principle that the divine encounters us through the visible, tangible, and physical realities of this life. Consequently instruments may be the means through which God encounters us. Instruments, it is argued, are never the source of God's grace, but they can be the sign of God's grace.

THE ORGAN IN WORSHIP

The best-known and most popular traditional instrument in worship is surely the organ. Most of us who come from churches that use the organ effectively probably think the use of it goes all the way back to the beginning of the church. Not so!

There was an organ in pagan times called the *hydraulis*, or water organ. It was used for pagan rites, the Roman games, and the theater. Consequently the church rejected its use!

When Rome fell, the organ fell with it and its sound was not heard in the West until the early Middle Ages. The organ continued to be used in the East, especially in the imperial courts of the Byzantine empire. In 757, Constantine, the Byzantine emperor, gave Pepin, the king of the Franks, an organ as a gift. The organ created an enormous amount of curiosity and interest.

Eventually the organ was incorporated into the life of the church, but the circumstances of its acceptance need to be understood to grasp why the church reversed its earlier rejection of the organ as a pagan instrument. It has to be understood that the medieval period was a new time in history. The church had conquered the pagan world, so to speak. The church was at the center of every village as a symbol of its central place in the whole world. The world had been Christianized. Everything had been redeemed and made new (so to speak), including the organ.

The worldview of the Middle Ages was strongly influenced by the Platonic concept of harmony. The harmony of the world and of society was also a Christian conviction. Harmony was considered an expression of closeness to God.

Music, particularly harmonious music, was viewed as an expression of God's harmony. The organ, it was observed, was the best instrument to express that harmony. The medieval church created a form of "Christian music" characterized by harmony. The clock, invented about the same time, represented the divine order of the heavens, while the organ represented divine harmony in music. The organ reached the zenith of its place in the church during the Renaissance. It became the central instrument in Protestant churches, reaching new heights of grandeur with J. S. Bach.

The centrality of the organ began to fade in the nineteenth century. Enlightenment thinkers scoffed at the idea that music was an expression of harmony and introduced the notion that music primarily exists to express human emotion and to provide entertainment and relaxation. In spite of these Enlightenment ideas about music, the organ remained the main musical instrument of the church and even came to epitomize sacred music in the nineteenth and early twentieth centuries.

In recent decades the use of the organ has declined due to the rise of contemporary instruments, a sound that first emerged in the general culture and then quickly found its way into the church. We will examine that issue in the next session.

WHAT DOES SOUND DO?

Sound is a very important part of life. There are sounds that we like and others that grate on our nerves. As I'm writing this material in the woods of Michigan, I can hear crickets, various birds, and bugs that I cannot name. Hearing all this makes me feel close to nature. Sometimes in the evening I turn off all the lights and sit in the dark on my screened-in porch and simply listen to the many sounds of nature. These sounds are restful and soothing to me.

In the same way, sound speaks to us in worship and declares the word of the Lord. The music expresses and proclaims the written text of God's word in Scripture and song. This sound speaks to us of God's forgiving and accepting grace, of God's love for us and for creation. It is an encountering sound, a formative influence in our spiritual walk with the Lord.

This sound may come from the organ, from other instruments, or even from movements in worship, as with the clanging of the cross, or the patter of feet, or the movement of the procession.

CONCLUSION

In this session we have encountered controversial issues. Should we use instruments in worship? Should the organ continue to have a place in our worship?

Objections raised by the early church fathers and John Calvin open some issues that we generally do not deal with. Their concept of a word-driven worship needs to be taken into account, and the later idea that sound, whether the sound of the voice or the sound of instruments, aids the communication of the word needs to be considered.

We will consider these issues further in later sessions.

STUDY GUIDE

Read Session 5, "Traditional Instruments in Worship,"
before answering these questions.

PART I: PERSONAL STUDY

Answer the following questions on your own.

1. *Life Connection*

♦ Describe a service of worship in which you participated where instruments were not used. Then describe a service in which instruments were used. What was the difference in your experience? _____

_____

_____

_____

2. *Content Questions*

♦ List the instruments used in the worship occasion described in 2 Chronicles 5:12–13. Try to imagine hearing the sound. Describe it. _____

_____

_____

_____

_____

♦ Psalm 150 names a number of instruments used in worship. Which of these are used in worship in your church?

Trumpet	❏ Yes	❏ No
Harp	❏ Yes	❏ No
Lyre	❏ Yes	❏ No
Strings	❏ Yes	❏ No
Flute	❏ Yes	❏ No
Tambourine	❏ Yes	❏ No
Cymbals	❏ Yes	❏ No

- Some Christian churches have objected to the use of instruments in worship. Use your own words to summarize their objections:

  a. _____

  _____

  b. _____

  _____

  c. _____

  _____

- Explain in your own words the theological argument for instrumentation in worship. _____

  _____

  _____

- Where do you personally stand on this issue? _____

  _____

  _____

- Summarize the history of the organ in terms of the following categories.

  Pagan use _____

  _____

  Byzantine use_____

  _____

  Medieval church _____

  _____

  Renaissance _____

  _____

  Nineteenth century_____

  _____

  Recent decades _____

  _____

- Why did the organ, which was rejected by the early church, find such acceptance in the medieval church? _____

  _____

  _____

- How did the Enlightenment understanding of music differ from the medieval understanding of music? _____

_____

_____

_____

_____

- Do you agree with the medieval or the Enlightenment view of music?
  ❑ Medieval   ❑ Enlightenment

- How do you think the Enlightenment view of music has affected music in our contemporary culture? Be as elaborate as possible in your evaluation. _____

_____

_____

_____

_____

_____

_____

3. *Application*

- Describe the effect that sound has on you. _____

_____

_____

_____

- What sounds in music lift your heart in worship? Are there sounds you sometimes hear in worship that are distracting? Describe. _____

_____

_____

_____

_____

PART II: GROUP DISCUSSION

Share the insights you gained from your personal study in Part I. Write out all answers that group members give to the questions on a chalkboard, a flip chart, or a dry erase board.

1. *Life Connection*

◆ Begin your study by inviting several members of the group to describe their response to worship situations where instrumentation was used and where instrumentation was not used.

2. *Content Questions*

◆ Ask group members to describe the sounds they hear when they reflect on 2 Chronicles 5:12–13.

◆ Compare the instrumentation found in Psalm 150 to the instrumentation used in your church.

◆ Select several simple, well-known songs to sing. Ask members of the group who play instruments to bring their instruments to class. Those who don't play instruments can pat their hands on their legs, whistle, beat a spoon against an object, or make some kind of harmonious sound as you sing. Spend as much time as you wish singing and sounding. Or you can spend some time just doing sound praise. When you are finished, talk about it. What did you experience?

◆ State each objection to the use of instruments in worship and discuss its pros and cons extensively.

◆ Deal with the incarnational significance of sound. Define the idea. Probe its meaning.

◆ Poll the class. How many think instrumentation has no place in worship? How many think instrumentation is vital to worship? Why?

◆ Briefly review the history of the organ in worship.

◆ Compare the medieval and Enlightenment views of music. Ask, Do you think the Enlightenment view of music has a place in worship?

- Discuss the role of sound in worship. Ask, What sounds release you to praise? What sounds hinder your worship?

3. *Application*

- Review the use of instrumentation in the worship of your church. List on a chalkboard all the instruments used over the course of a year. List how many Sundays each instrument is used. What instruments are never used? What does this self-evaluation say to you about the role of instruments in your worship?

- Plan a worship service that uses all the instruments played by various people in your church. Follow the fourfold pattern of gathering, hearing the word, celebrating at the table, and sending forth. What instruments best express the mood and purpose of each part of worship?

- How has this study of instruments in worship enriched your experience of worship?

MUSIC, WORSHIP, AND CONTEMPORARY CULTURE

A Study in Contemporary Praise Music

After I completed a workshop on worship renewal a few years ago, a young, earnest man came to me and said, "You make worship renewal too hard." I was curious about his remark and wanted to know more. "What do you mean?" I said, hoping he would be able to pinpoint the problem he had with my presentation. "Well, in our church we got into worship renewal in fifteen minutes." "How so?" I responded in astonishment. "We put our chairs in a circle, brought in a person with a guitar to teach us the new choruses, and there we were—experiencing worship renewal."

There are two assumptions in this young man's statement that relate to contemporary music, worship, and culture. The first is that worship is primarily music; the second is that renewal is linked with contemporary instrumentation. Let's look at these assumptions by examining the rise of contemporary music and worship and its relationship to the general culture.

CONTEMPORARY MUSIC, WORSHIP, AND CULTURE

There is no question that the Western world has gone through very significant cultural changes since World War II. The old worldview was more rigid, more structured, more determined by the accepted rules of society than is our present one. In the old world, music and worship were quite predictable. Each denomination had its own style and form of music and worship.

Culture began to change after 1960, shifting from a staid and predictable society to an "anything goes" people. New, innovative styles characterized clothing, music, cars, houses, and decorations. Spouse-swapping, sexual permissiveness, and a do-your-own-thing philosophy became widely accepted. Musical styles exploded with Elvis Presley, the Beatles, hard rock, and rap.

These cultural developments were bound to make an impact on the church. The classical medieval view of music as reflecting cosmic harmony had already given way to a more personal concept of emotional expression and entertainment. The music of the 1960s and beyond clearly expressed this new motif, which also began to find expression in Christian music.

This shift in Christian music first appeared in the music of Bill and Gloria Gaither. Recently I spoke with Bill Gaither about the music in the early 1960s and beyond. He had this to say: "You know, Bob, when Gloria and I first started our concerts we thought we were doing a performance for the people. When we sang 'There's a sweet spirit in this place and I know that it's the Spirit of the Lord' the people began to sing along with us. Then they took this music home to their churches, and with that the praise-chorus phenomenon began."

The praise worship phenomenon received a second push forward in the Jesus movement of the early 1970s. When the hippie movement of the 1960s began to lose steam, a lot of the hippies moved to the beaches of southern California, hung out together, smoked pot, played their guitars, and sang the music of revolution.

A faithful pastor, Chuck Smith of Costa Mesa, California, made his way to the beaches and introduced these hippies to Jesus. One by one they became Christians and made their way to Smith's church. One of these hippies was Tommy Coombs, now one of the owners of Maranatha! Music. Tommy told me he was looking for God in all the wrong places. Someone came to him and said, "Tommy, God dwells in this local church [the church pastored by Chuck Smith]. Come with me and meet God." This church had become a haven for hippies. They brought their guitars and sang new songs they had written from the Scriptures about loving, worshiping, and serving God. So Tommy came. And Tommy told me, "When I opened the door of that church and walked into the sound of that singing, I knew I was home. I had found God. There God was, dwelling in the midst of the people, enthroned through their songs of praise."

The Jesus movement soon spread across the nation and around the world. And with the spread of the Jesus music came a new genre of praise music, guitars, and contemporary instruments. Contemporary music and worship are here to stay and have continued to spread.

HOW TO EVALUATE CONTEMPORARY MUSIC AND WORSHIP

The contemporary music and worship phenomenon needs to be evaluated in terms of its relationship to contemporary culture. Clearly contemporary worship is an expression of culture. It uses popular instruments such as drums, guitars, and synthesizers. It produces the same kind of sound, and it is geared toward emotional response and entertainment.

The argument for using contemporary music in worship is that it reaches the people of this culture with the gospel. It is an indisputable fact that contemporary churches are growing. They do appeal to the younger generation and they do reach them with the saving message of Christ.

The argument against contemporary music is drawn from the early church fathers and John Calvin (see Session 5). No one disputes that contemporary worship is an accommodation to the current cultural style. It follows the genre of pagan music and produces, in some cases, the sounds that celebrate the chaos of a world without God.

Marshall McLuhan coined the phrase, "the medium is the message." If that phrase is applied to contemporary music in worship, it implies that the message communicated is more than the words. The words may be about the peace, harmony, and relationship found in Jesus Christ, but the sound may send messages of confusion, chaos, and terror. For this reason contemporary music in worship walks a thin line.

Contemporary worship is generally interpreted in terms of music. Chuck Fromm of Maranatha! Music captured it well when he said to me, "Face it, Bob. The new sacrament is music." He was being critical of the contemporary worship movement when he made his statement.

In contemporary circles, as was the case with the young fellow who chided me for making worship too difficult, worship is equated with singing and music. Most contemporary churches are characterized by a twofold pattern of worship. The first half hour consists of singing, and the second half is preaching. Contemporary churches refer to the Sunday service as a time of worship and a time of teaching. This is a truncated understanding of worship. It fails to recognize that the two foci of Christian worship, going all the way back to the early church, are the apostolic teaching and the breaking of the bread (see Acts 2:42). These two actions proclaim and enact the living, dying, and rising of Christ as well as the overthrow of the powers of evil.

God ordained word and table as the chief vehicles for the communication of God's grace. Music is not a primary communicator of grace. But it is a secondary communicator of God's grace. Therefore music does have a sacramental quality (a means through which the divine is encountered), but it is not one of the chief sacraments of the church.

In the past, Catholics made the Eucharist the primary communicator of grace, while Protestants made preaching the primary communicator of grace. The contemporary church makes music the primary communicator of grace. The issue here for all of us is to achieve wholeness and completeness. The fullness of worship is found in word, sacrament, music, prayer, confession, fellowship, and the like. To assume that music or the word alone or the Eucharist alone bears the whole of worship is a view that is out of keeping with the biblical record and the witness of history.

TOWARD BALANCE

The current worship scene is polarized. On one side are the traditionalist churches and on the other side are the contemporary churches. Is there any way the two can work together?

The cultural distinction may be helpful at least in appreciating each other's perspective. Advocates of contemporary worship should be able to appreciate the concern for the harmony of God's universe as expressed in traditional worship; traditional Christians should be able to appreciate the concern for contemporary relevance and the emotional support that music can provide. Simply seeing matters from each other's perspective and reaching out to understand each other is a start.

I like to think that adapting the principles of music and worship used in the early church would be of great value to the current debate. The music and worship of the early church existed before the development of specifically Christian music based on the medieval notion of harmony. The music of the early church combined both hymnology and the more spontaneous Jubilation. The early church affirmed the transcendence of God and used music in a way that promoted a strong sense of awe and reverence; it also drew on *jubilus* and affirmed the significance of an intimate relationship with God that can be experienced in worship.

Drawing on the perspective of the early church can help us deal creatively with the relationship between music, worship, and culture. Today's church may not want to go as far as the early church fathers did, outlawing contemporary instruments and sound. On the other hand their concerns may help today's church ask some critical questions about the accommodation of church music to contemporary rock and pop styles.

CONCLUSION

The issue of music, worship, and culture is as hot today as it has ever been in the history of the church. Instead of dividing up in sides that blast away at one another and disregard each other's insights and ministry, we need to come together in humility and genuine concern for the unity of the church. The answer is not to perpetuate division in the church but to find new and creative ways of working together to create a style of worship that incorporates both the old and the new.

STUDY GUIDE

*Read Session 6, "Music, Worship, and Contemporary Culture,"
before answering these questions.*

PART I: PERSONAL STUDY

Answer the following questions on your own.

1. *Life Connection*

♦ Have you ever participated in a praise and worship service? This kind of service is characterized by contemporary instrumentation, and by choruses that range in style from folk to soft rock. If so, describe that service below. If not, try to attend this kind of service as you study this topic.

_____

_____

_____

2. *Content Questions*

♦ Answer the following questions to review the background of contemporary praise music:

Describe the style of music that predominated before World War II and the style that predominated after it. _____

_____

Describe the cultural changes of the 1960s. _____

_____

How did these cultural changes influence the church? _____

_____

What were the historical origins of the praise music phenomenon?

_____

_____

◆ Evaluate contemporary music in worship by answering the following questions:

What is the argument for contemporary music in worship? _____

_____

_____

What is the argument against contemporary music in worship? _____

_____

_____

Explain how it is that contemporary Christian music walks a thin line.

_____

_____

How do you respond to the statement, "The new sacrament is music"?

_____

What twofold pattern of worship is used in many contemporary churches?

_____

_____

How does the twofold pattern of worship compare with the fourfold patter studied in earlier sessions? _____

_____

_____

_____

◆ Identify the primary means of the communication of God's grace in each
of the following worship communities:
Catholic _____

_____

Protestant _____

_____

Contemporary _____

_____

- Describe what is involved in the fullness of worship. _____

  _____

  _____

- State what can we appreciate from:
  Traditional worship _____

  _____

  Contemporary worship _____

  _____

- Explain how the music of the early church provides a pattern for the future use of music in worship. _____

  _____

  _____

3. *Application*

- What perspective on the issue of music in the church today have you gained as a result of this study? _____

  _____

  _____

PART II: GROUP DISCUSSION

Share the insights you gained from your personal study in Part I. Write out all answers that group members give to the questions on a chalkboard, a flip chart, or a dry erase board.

1. *Life Connection*

- If yours is a traditional church, ask members of the group who have participated in a praise and worship service to describe their experience. If yours is a praise and worship church, ask those who have participated in a traditional worship to describe their experience.

2. *Thought Questions*

- Compare culture before World War II with culture since World War II. You may want to use two columns on a chalkboard to show the cultural shift.

- Discuss the culture of the 1960s. What kind of changes occurred in this decade? Write these changes on the board.
- How has the postwar culture and especially the 1960s culture affected the church? Write these answers on the board.
- Identify members of the group who remember the historical origins of the praise movement. Ask them to recall their impressions.
- Review the arguments for and against contemporary praise. Poll the group not for the purpose of argument but to find out the general disposition of the group. (Do not let the discussion degenerate into a divisive experience.)
- What is the thin line that contemporary Christian music walks?
- Describe services in which the focus of an encounter with God is the word preached, the Eucharist celebrated, or the music sung.
- What can traditionalists learn from contemporary worship? What can contemporary worship learn from traditionalists?

3. *Application*

- Evaluate the use of contemporary choruses in your church. Are they overused, underused, or in balance?
- Plan a worship service that blends hymns and choruses. A good musical resource is *Renew! Songs and Hymns for Blended Worship* (Hope Publishing, 1996).

MUSIC IN THE FUTURE OF CHRISTIAN WORSHIP

A Study of Music in Blended Worship

 I have already mentioned that I grew up in a minister's home. My father specialized in the prophetic literature of the Bible and often spoke at prophetic conferences. He frequently made predictions about the future. I was always a little skeptical about these forecasts and generally thought that history was best interpreted after the fact.

Similarly, I feel somewhat tentative about predictions regarding worship. I believe that the future of worship will remain pluralistic, but that there will be a strong movement toward blending traditional and contemporary worship.

In this session I want to look at how music may look in blended worship. I'll use the fourfold pattern of early Christian worship, which has been restored in the present renewal of traditional worship.

MUSIC FOR THE GATHERING

The purpose of the gathering is to bring people into the presence of God and to prepare them to hear the word of the Lord. Music serves this purpose, it does not dominate it.

The mood of the gathering is one of joy and celebration. This mood is generally established by the music and the songs selected. A sense of joyfulness can be accomplished through either traditional joyful hymns or contemporary choruses, or, as in the case of blended worship, a combination of both.

As people gather and find their seats, the service may use a traditional organ prelude, a set of sung contemporary choruses, or both. Once people have gathered, an entrance hymn with a procession can be used to express the congregation's spiritual entrance before the very throne of God. The entrance hymn should be a hymn, not a song or a chorus. A hymn with good content signals the enthronement of God upon the praises of the people.

The hymn may be followed by a call to worship and an invocation of God's presence. Now that the congregation has gathered around the throne of God, it is appropriate to sing praises to God. The congregation may sing a traditional act of praise such as the Gloria in Excelsis Deo, or a set of praise songs, or both.

The gathering is brought to closure with a confession of sin (like Isaiah's confession, "Woe to me . . . I am a man of unclean lips" (Isa 6:5). Then a prayer may be said as a segue into the service of the word.

Here is a summary of the role of music in a blended gathering:

- Organ prelude or a set of choruses
- Traditional processional hymn
- Call to worship
- Invocation
- Act of praise such as the Gloria in Excelsis Deo, or a set of praise choruses, or a combination of both
- Confession
- Opening prayer

THE SERVICE OF THE WORD

The purpose of the service of the word is quite different from the purpose of the gathering. The people have gathered to be addressed by the word. So the purpose of this part of the service is to take up residence within God's people and to shape them into Christlikeness.

Because the purpose has changed, the mood changes as well—to quiet and meditative listening and responding. Music serves this purpose by helping drive the word home and assisting the congregation in the act of receiving God's word. Music also assists the congregation in its response to God's word.

The service of the word begins with the reading of Scripture. In traditional churches, especially those that follow the lectionary, there are three Scripture readings. Between the readings the church sings in response to the word (this tradition goes back to the ancient synagogue and to the subsequent practice of the early church). While contemporary churches do not read as much Scripture as traditional churches, most contemporary churches do read at least one and perhaps two Scriptures.

The music between the readings is normally a psalm of response. The resurgence of psalm singing has produced a number of alternatives in style. A church may choose to sing a psalm in metrical, chant, responsorial, or chorus style.

The song sung before the Gospel reading is often an alleluia, which may be traditional or contemporary, or may be from Africa, Asia, the Caribbean, or other parts of the world. The alleluias express the joy of the people at hearing the gospel.

Music that follows the sermon generally elicits a response from the people. Again, a broad range is available. The music may reflect the particular theological background of the church. Some churches may prefer songs of invitation or dedication; other churches may prefer sung statements of faith, such as the Nicene Creed or a hymn of confessing faith. There are also choruses of confessing faith that can be used after the sermon as well.

Here is a possible order of worship:

- Old Testament reading
- A sung psalm
- Epistle reading
- A sung alleluia
- Gospel reading
- Sermon
- Sung response, such as invitation, dedication, or confession of faith
- Prayers of the people (in some traditions prayers are sung)
- Passing of the peace (announcements and offering may follow)

The Service of Thanksgiving

In the fourfold pattern of worship, the word, with readings and preaching, is second. The third part of worship is the response to the word, the thanksgiving or, to use a more colloquial term, the thank-you the church gives to God for Jesus Christ and his saving and healing work.

Traditionally the church's thanksgiving is the Eucharist (from the Greek word for "thanksgiving"). While most liturgical churches celebrate the Eucharist weekly (as did the early church), most Protestant churches celebrate the Lord's Supper on the first Sunday of the month.

Protestant churches are experiencing a growing commitment toward a more frequent practice of the Eucharist. Since it is a stretch for most Protestant churches to celebrate the Eucharist weekly, many churches are adopting the practice of an alternative time of thanks. Therefore I will address both music in the Eucharist and music in the alternative form of thanksgiving.

THE EUCHARIST

The Eucharist may begin with an invitation to Communion song. The minister begins the prayers at the table by inviting members of the congregation to lift their hearts to heaven and gather around the throne of God with the heavenly host. At this point the congregation sings a "Holy, Holy, Holy" (Sanctus). The prayer commemorating the work of Christ and giving thanks for his saving work follows. The prayer moves into the words of institution, the remembrance, and the acclamation "Christ has died, Christ has risen, Christ will come again" (which may be sung). Then comes the prayer for the Holy Spirit's presence (epiklēsis), followed by the Lord's Prayer (may be sung) and the invitation to receive the bread and wine. This may include a sung "Christ our Passover is sacrificed for us." While the procedure varies from church to church, our interest here is in the Communion music.

Renewal worship has shifted from a dour, funereal experience of Communion (established by slow and sober organ music) to a time of unitive singing. This singing follows the text of death, resurrection, and exaltation or of an intimate, meditative relationship with God. The choice of music during the reception of bread and wine is of utmost importance because it shapes the spiritual experience of the community.

The traditional and the contemporary may be mixed, for example, by focusing on death with "When I Survey the Wondrous Cross" followed by a contemporary song, such as the Taizé "Jesus, Remember Me." The resurrection motif may be captured in choruses such as the Taizé "Gloria" or the well-known "He Is Lord." An exaltation motif may be captured in Twila Paris's song "He Is Exalted."

Here is a possible outline of the Eucharist:

- Song of invitation to Communion
- Preface prayer ending in a sung "Holy, Holy, Holy"
- Prayer of thanksgiving
- Words of institution
- Words of remembrance
- Sung acclamation ("Christ has died," etc.)
- Prayer for the Holy Spirit

- Lord's Prayer (may be sung)
- Invitation to receive ("Christ our Passover")
- Communion songs during reception, including songs of death, resurrection, and exaltation, or songs of intimate relationship ("I Love You, Lord") and reflection ("Of the Father's Love Begotten")

The Alternative Time of Thanksgiving

The alternative time of thanksgiving is gaining great support among churches that do not celebrate Communion every Sunday. It provides the church with an opportunity to give thanks and sing relational songs to God. Churches may use this time for testimony, joys and concerns, prayers of thanksgiving, and singing. The singing may focus on the Christian's relationship with the triune God.

In this way the alternative time of thanksgiving can be similar to the Eucharist experience. The Eucharist is ordered by (1) praise to the Father, (2) commemoration of the work of the Son, and (3) invocation of the Holy Spirit. Traditional and contemporary songs may be directed toward the triune God or, as in the Eucharist, songs of meditation and relationship may be sung.

Here is a possible order for the alternative time of thanksgiving:

- A song of invitation to give thanks (e.g., "Give Thanks with a Grateful Heart")
- Testimonials of thanks for what God is doing in the life of this or that person or in the church
- Prayers of thanksgiving
- A time of singing songs that praise the Father, remember the works of the Son, and invoke the presence of the Holy Spirit; or songs of meditation, thankfulness, and relationship

The Service of Dismissal

Worship always ends with a sending forth. The traditional dismissal includes a benediction (pronouncing God's blessing upon the people), a dismissal song, and the closing words ("Go forth into the world to love and serve the Lord," to which the people respond, "Thanks be to God"). Many sung benedictions, both traditional and contemporary, are available in hymnbooks and musical resources. A gospel song may be sung as a dismissal hymn. Gospel songs have to do with going forth, telling others, and living the Christian life.

Here is a possible order for the dismissal:

- Benediction (may be sung)
- Dismissal gospel song
- Words of dismissal

CONCLUSION

I have attempted in this fourfold pattern of worship to show you how to combine traditional and contemporary music. I have said nothing about instruments, but I am assuming that traditional hymns will be led by the organ and contemporary songs by a guitar, a piano, a synthesizer, or a praise band with several worship leaders at appropriately placed microphones. What I have given you is not a rigid prescription. It is a description that you need to adapt to your own heritage and culture.

STUDY GUIDE

*Read Session 7, "Music in the Future of Christian Worship,"
before answering these questions.*

PART I: PERSONAL STUDY

Answer the following questions on your own.

1. *Life Connection*

• Make your own prediction regarding the future of Christian worship and
  the place of music in worship. Base it on observation and experience as
  well as a gut-level feeling about what's happening in the culture and in
  the church. _____

  _____

  _____

  _____

  _____

2. *Content Questions*

• What is the purpose of the gathering? _____

  _____

  _____

  _____

• What is the mood of the gathering? _____

  _____

  _____

  _____

• How do the acts of worship in the gathering reflect both its purpose and
  its mood? _____

  _____

  _____

  _____

◆ Write the acts of gathering in the column on the left. In the column on the right, state how these acts of gathering actually accomplish the purpose of bringing people into the presence of God and readying them to hear the word of the Lord.

Acts of Gathering   How Each Act Functions

_____   _____

_____   _____

_____   _____

_____   _____

_____   _____

_____   _____

_____   _____

◆ Describe how an entrance hymn and a song of praise differ in content.

Entrance hymn _____

_____

Song of praise _____

_____

◆ What are the purpose and the mood of the service of the word?

Purpose _____

Mood _____

_____

◆ How do the acts of worship in the service of the word reflect the purpose and the mood of worship? _____

_____

_____

◆ For each kind of music sung in the service of the word, explain the purpose and mood.

Music	Purpose and Mood
Psalms	_____
	_____
	_____
Alleluias	_____
	_____
	_____
Invitation songs	_____
	_____
	_____
Songs of faith confession	_____
	_____
	_____

◆ Describe the two types of thanksgiving that the church offers to God.

a. _____

_____

_____

b. _____

_____

_____

◆ What are the purpose and the mood of the time of thanksgiving?

Purpose _____

_____

_____

Mood _____

_____

_____

◆ Here is a list of the kinds of songs sung at the Eucharist. How does each song represent our posture before God in worship?

Eucharist Songs	What Each Represents
Invitation to Communion	_____
Sanctus	_____
The acclamation	_____
The Lord's Prayer	_____
Christ our Passover	_____
Communion song	_____
Death	_____
Resurrection	_____
Exaltation song, or	_____
Relational song	_____
Closing song	_____

◆ Here is a list of songs sung in the alternative service of thanksgiving. How does each song express our relationship to God?

Alternative Songs	What Each Expresses
Set of songs to	
Father	_____
Son	_____
Spirit	_____
Set of Songs of	
Thankfulness	_____
Relationship	_____

◆ What are the purpose and the mood of the service of dismissal?

Purpose _____

_____

Mood _____

_____

- What elements of the service of dismissal may be sung? _____

_____

_____

_____

3. *Application*

- Imagine in your heart and mind any one of the following acts of worship, then spend some time imagining your way through it musically.

The gathering
The service of the word
The Eucharist
The alternative thanksgiving

PART II: GROUP DISCUSSION

Share the insights you gained from your personal study in Part I. Write out all answers that group members give to the questions on a chalkboard, a flip chart, or a dry erase board.

1. *Life Connection*

- Ask several members of the group to share how they envision the future of Christian worship and to explain why.

2. *Content Questions*

- Spend some time probing and discussing the gathering. Discuss, perhaps even debate such questions as:

What is its purpose?
What is its mood?
What is its structure?
How is music used in the gathering?
What is the spiritual experience of the people in the gathering?

- Evaluate the gathering in the worship of your church. Should your gathering be changed in any way?

- Spend some time probing and discussing the service of the word. Discuss and debate the following:

  What is its purpose?
  What is its mood?
  What is its structure?
  How is music used in the service of the word?
  What is the spiritual experience of the people in the service of the word?

- Spend some time probing and discussing the service of the Eucharist. Discuss and debate the following:

  What is its purpose?
  What is its mood?
  What is its structure?
  How is music used in the Eucharist?
  What is the spiritual experience of the people in the Eucharist?

- Spend some time reflecting on the alternative service of thanksgiving.

  What is its purpose?
  What is its mood?
  What is its structure?
  How is music used in the alternative time of thanksgiving?
  What is the spiritual experience of the people in this time?

- Spend some time reflecting on the dismissal.

  What is its purpose?
  What is its mood?
  What is its structure?
  How is music used in the dismissal?
  What is the spiritual experience of the people in this time?

3. *Application*

- Evaluate the music of each of the four parts of worship in your church. How does the music help you experience the gathering, the word, the time of thanks (both in Eucharist and alternative thanks) and the sending forth?

- Plan music for each part of worship. Do so with input from what you have learned in this session. Carefully choose your music to lead you into the experience intended in each part of worship.
- How has this session enriched your experience of music in worship?

PART II

~~~~~~~

THE ARTS IN

WORSHIP

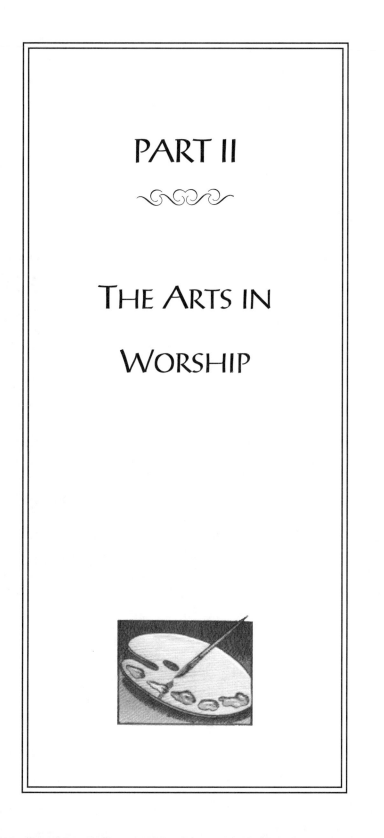

THE ROLE OF THE ARTS
IN WORSHIP

A Study in How God Communicates

Let me tell you about two different but very memorable experiences of worship. A few years ago on Pentecost Sunday I attended worship in a downtown church in the city of Moscow. The service was fully ablaze with the presence of God's glory, communicated through the arts. Every square inch of the interior of that great cathedral was covered with icons and frescos in bold and imaginative colors. The risen Christ in the dome reigned over his entire creation. The worship celebrants, with their colorful vestments, looked like the twenty-four elders before the throne of God. Numerous flickering candles, together with the sound of the choir and more than five thousand eager worshipers packed into that space, gave a feeling of being in heaven itself!

Shortly thereafter I had an opportunity to visit a Plymouth Brethren church. If you know anything about the Plymouth Brethren, you know that they are champions of plainness in space and decor as well as dress, speech, and lifestyle. In that clapboard building without any visual art I was engaged with this community in a memorable experience of worship at word and table.

So why the arts? Before I begin to answer that question I want to make it clear that the arts are not necessary for worship. Even music is not necessary for worship. Worship needs only the people gathered around the word and the table in spirit and in truth, praising God, remembering the saving work of God's Son, Jesus Christ, and calling upon the Holy Spirit.

So why the arts?

THE BIBLICAL BASIS

The biblical basis for the arts in worship is found in the Old Testament, particularly in the instructions for building Solomon's temple. The temple was a visual symbol of the presence of God among the people of Israel, and it was clearly majestic inside and out. David said, "The house to be built for the LORD should be of great magnificence and fame and splendor in the sight of all the nations" (1 Chron 22:5). He charged Solomon,

> I have taken great pains to provide for the temple of the LORD a hundred thousand talents of gold, a million talents of silver, quantities of bronze and iron too great to be weighed, and wood and stone. And you may add to them. You have many workmen: stonecutters, masons and carpenters, as well as men skilled in every kind of work in gold and silver, bronze and iron—craftsmen beyond number. Now begin the work, and the LORD be with you. (1 Chron 22:14–16)

THE THEOLOGICAL BASIS

Those who argue in favor of the arts in worship do so from the perspective of creation and incarnation. The doctrine of creation affirms the goodness of all material things, including gold, silver, wood, masonry, and the like.

They argue that through creation we know that God is creative and beautiful. Consequently, when human effort is applied to the raw materials of creation to build a place of beauty where the character and acts of God are proclaimed and enacted, the God of creation is experienced in the very stuff of the created order.

They go one step further to argue that by virtue of the incarnation, creation is ever affirmed as a means through which God can be known and experienced.

Thus the incarnational argument for the arts in worship is simply this: God communicates through the visible and the tangible. Because God encountered us in the flesh and blood of the man Jesus, we can affirm that an encounter with the divine can occur through the material. God principally encounters us through the book—the Bible—and through the sacred action of water, bread, and wine. Thus, the argument goes, God can also (secondarily) encounter us through the material reality of the arts.

OBJECTIONS

Those who object to the use of the arts in worship employ several arguments. First, they argue that God had to use visible objects as a form of communication in the Old Testament because an inner spiritual consciousness had not yet fully developed. But, goes the argument, when the spiritual state of humanity had developed adequately to grasp the realm of the supernatural, there was no longer any need for physical, visual communication. Communication between God and humanity became spiritual.

Second, the Gnostics (a heretical sect) argued that the physical world is intrinsically evil. They interpreted Paul's reference to "the world, the flesh, and the devil" as a negative reference to the created order itself. Consequently they completely rejected anything physical in the Christian faith and even argued that the incarnation was not real, but a spiritual appearance or an apparition. The church totally rejected this view.

Third, the Puritans and other Protestants argued against the arts in worship on the basis of the Second Commandment, "You shall not make for yourself an idol in the form of anything in heaven above or on the earth beneath or in the waters below" (Exod 20:4). It must be admitted that this verse is difficult to interpret and apply. Certainly it means that no art object is to be worshiped. But does it negate the incarnational principle that God encounters us through visible, tangible means? Does God speak through the arrangement of space, the contours of the cross, the visual experience of processions and banners? These are some of the knotty questions raised by the Second Commandment.

A final argument against the use of the visual arts in worship begins with the New Testament's use of the temple as a symbol of the worshiping church, the new Jerusalem where God dwells in the midst of his people (Rev 21:1–3). The teaching that Old Testament ceremonial practices are fulfilled in Jesus Christ (as in Heb 9:1–10:18) is taken to mean that all ceremony is now superseded.

Supporters of the arts in worship counter that while sacrifices of the Old Testament were fulfilled in Jesus Christ, artistic beauty and the ceremonial may continue as forms through which the divine is encountered.

Clearly arguments exist on both sides of the question. But historically the greater part of the church has supported the arts. Today's renewal of worship includes a decided renaissance of the arts in worship.

THE ARTS AS A VEHICLE OF COMMUNICATION

Why the arts in worship? They are vehicles for communication. The arts are not venerated or worshiped. Rather, they are used to communicate truth about God.

Let's go back again to my experience in the Orthodox cathedral in Moscow. This cathedral, of course, represents the zenith of the arts in worship. By using this example, I am not telling you to erect icons in your church or redo your walls with frescos. What I am saying is that the arts in that setting were so alive that my whole person was engaged in worship. My eyes saw, my ears heard, my nose smelled, my body moved, my emotions were full, my heart was lifted up, my will was challenged. The arts engage the whole person—body, soul, spirit, senses—in worship.

RULES FOR USING THE ARTS IN WORSHIP

Let's remember that worship is the communal action of the church in which the people of God proclaim and enact the historical death and resurrection of Christ. In this worship they also anticipate the final consummation when the powers of evil will be put away forever. God will then reign in the new heavens and the new earth. Rules for the arts within worship must be laid out with this biblical understanding of worship in mind. There are three basic rules for the arts in worship:

- Art should be characterized by simplicity. It should not be smothered by explanation and an abundance of words, which destroy the mystery. Nor should it be so complex that the message remains hidden and obscure.

- Art should be well executed. When music, drama, dance, or environ-mental symbols such as banners are shoddy, they reflect poorly on the message they represent. When characterized by excellence, they express the beauty, the majesty, and the mystery of God.

- Art should be integrated with the flow of worship. Art in worship is not a performance directed toward the people; rather, art supports the acts of gathering, hearing the word, giving thanks, and sending forth.

CONCLUSION

Our brief study argues in favor of a place for the arts in worship. This argument is based on the Old Testament aesthetic premise and on the doctrines of creation and incarnation. Art in worship serves the action of worship. Art itself is never worshiped. It serves the message it proclaims.

STUDY GUIDE

Read Session 8, "The Role of the Arts in Worship,"
before answering these questions.

PART I: PERSONAL STUDY

Answer the following questions on your own.

1. *Life Connection*
   * Recall an experience of worship that was alive with the arts. How did God encounter you through the arts?_____

   _____

   _____

   _____

2. *Content Questions*
   * Read the whole of 1 Chronicles 22. How do you think 1 Chronicles 22:19 may be used to support the use of the arts in worship?

   _____

   _____

   _____

   _____

   * Summarize in your own words the argument for the arts in worship drawn from the doctrine of creation. _____

   _____

   _____

   _____

   * Explain in your own words the incarnational argument for the use of the arts in worship. _____

   _____

   _____

   _____

- In the column of the left, list the four arguments against the use of the arts. On the right, indicate your response to these arguments.

  Arguments against the Use   My Response
     of the Arts in Worship
  _____

  1. _____   _____
     _____   _____
  2. _____   _____
     _____   _____
  3. _____   _____
     _____   _____
  4. _____   _____
     _____   _____

- Read Hebrews 9:1–10:18. Do you interpret this passage as for or against ceremonial worship?   ❏ For   ❏ Against
  Explain: _____
  _____
  _____
  _____

- How are the arts used in worship according to the author of this study?
  _____
  _____
  _____

- How do the arts assist worship? _____
  _____
  _____
  _____

- Summarize the biblical definition of worship in your own words.
  _____
  _____
  _____

- State and briefly explain in your own words the three basic rules for the arts in worship.

Three basic rules	My explanation of these rules
1. _____	_____
_____	_____
_____	_____
2. _____	_____
_____	_____
_____	_____
3. _____	_____
_____	_____
_____	_____

3. *Application*
- Briefly summarize your own convictions about the use of the arts in worship.

  _____
  _____
  _____

PART II: GROUP DISCUSSION

Share the insights you gained from your personal study in Part I. Write out all answers that group members give to the questions on a chalkboard, a flip chart, or a dry erase board.

1. *Life Connection*
- Begin your session by asking several people to share their experiences of worship alive with the arts. Be sure to explore how the arts served worship and communicated God's truth. If the action described was a performance, explore how that affected the experience of worship.

2. *Thought Questions*

◆ Read 1 Chronicles 22. Ask group members to share their response to this passage. Find a picture of the temple or a plan of its design and bring it to class.

◆ Discuss the argument for the arts based in the theology of creation and incarnation. Ask for examples of how God may be encountered in creation or through some material object.

◆ Discuss the arguments against the use of the arts in worship. Ask the group members to respond to each argument.

◆ Read through Hebrews 9:1–10:18. Discuss how this passage may be interpreted for or against ceremonial worship.

◆ Discuss the author's comments that the arts are a vehicle for communication. Ask, If God speaks through the arts, can you give an illustration of how God spoke and communicated to you through the arts?

3. *Application*

◆ Evaluate the use of the arts in the worship of your church using the three basic rules for the arts.

◆ Discuss how the three basic rules for the arts may influence the use of the arts in your church.

◆ How has this study helped you understand the use of the arts in worship?

THE PRIMARY
WORSHIP ENVIRONMENT

A Study in Assembly, Pulpit, and Table

 I have just returned from a two-week tour of England, and memories of the great churches and cathedrals of the past are still vivid in my mind.

As I entered the great cathedrals of England—Canterbury, Westminster Abbey, St. Paul's—I felt the need to be quiet, to meditate, to look, to hear, and to feel the majesty and mystery of God in that place.

I recall a statement someone made to me once. "You know," he said, "in some churches you just want to drop to your knees and be silent before God; in other churches you simply want to chatter." I thought his point was quite apt, for I have had similar experiences in various church spaces. This suggests that environment has a lot to do with worship. Someone has said that "we shape our environment, then our environment shapes us." How true! In this session we want to address the role of the environment in worship.

BIBLICAL AND THEOLOGICAL ASSUMPTIONS

Before we begin to address the role of the physical environment in worship, we need to set out some biblical and theological principles that will guide our discussion.

- The church is the people of God. Let's remember that the church is not the building and not the denomination. The church comes into being when the people assemble to worship.

- The building in which the people assemble is primarily the house of the people. God does not dwell in a building. God dwells in the people who gather in the building. Nevertheless, we can meaningfully speak of the place where we meet as God's house because God's presence seems somehow to abide in the place where the people meet with God.

* Worship is primarily the work that people do, not their environment. The people remember, proclaim, enact, and anticipate the saving deeds of God. Thus the environment serves the action of the people but does not constitute the action itself.

PRIMARY SYMBOLS OF THE WORSHIP ENVIRONMENT

The primary symbols of the worship environment are those visible and tangible realities through which the gospel is proclaimed and enacted. The two primary symbols are:

* The body gathered in a particular space. Since worship has to do with experiencing the saving presence of Christ, the assembled people should sit in a configuration that allows them to see each other and to participate with each other as they worship. Above all, the seating arrangement should allow the people to see, hear, and move.

* The furniture of worship. The furniture of worship speaks to the presence of Christ in the assembled body. This furniture should be placed in such a way that each piece effectively communicates its symbolic meaning. Four pieces of furniture are classed as primary symbols:

  The baptismal font or pool. Since this piece of furniture represents entry into the church, its best location is near the entrance door.

  The pulpit. A freestanding pulpit—near the table and in a place where everyone can see it—reflects the revelation of God's word.

  The table. A freestanding table—near the pulpit and visible to all—speaks of the death and resurrection of Christ.

  The presider's chair. A freestanding chair placed behind the pulpit and the table speaks to the position of Christ who presides over the assembly through the one who delivers the word, celebrates Communion, and baptizes in his name. (This symbol is used by churches presided over by bishops, such as the Orthodox, the Catholic, and the Episcopal churches.)

SECONDARY SYMBOLS OF THE WORSHIP ENVIRONMENT

The secondary symbols of the presence of Christ in worship are the objects that speak of redemption. They are secondary because they do not hold the same necessity for worship signified by the primary symbols. These objects include books, such as the Gospel book or lectionary books, candles, crosses, Communion vessels, banners, linens, vestments, and flowers. We will deal with these secondary symbols in Session 10.

THE WORSHIP ENVIRONMENT DURING VARIOUS SEASONS OF THE CHRISTIAN YEAR

In addition to the primary and secondary symbols of the presence of Christ, the environment includes symbols that speak the particular biblical mood of each season of the Christian year.

- Advent. At one time Advent was understood as a penitential season. While penitence in preparation for the coming of Christ is still a part of Advent, it should be seen as a season of joyous anticipation. The Advent wreath with its five candles is the most obvious object to be included in the environment for this season.

- Christmas. The festivity of Christmas, the birth of Christ, is expressed by flowers—poinsettias and greenery. The Christmas crib or manger scenes should be located in a place where they can be seen, but not before the table or pulpit, where they distract from the major symbols of worship.

- Epiphany. The manifestation of Jesus to the world on Epiphany, January 6, ends the Christmas season. As such, January 6 employs the same environmental motif of Christmas. The season after Epiphany is ordinary or nonfestive time and should conform to the environment of that time.

- Lent. Lent prepares worshipers for the events of Holy Week and is a season of austerity, reflecting the sobriety of repentance.

- Holy Week. The celebration of the triduum—the three days of Maundy Thursday, Good Friday, and the Great Paschal Vigil—should be seen as one continuous event. This event is dominated by the special symbols of these liturgies—bread, wine, the washing of feet, stripping of the church, solemn processions, light, fire, water, and the cross.

- Easter. The joyful season of Easter is symbolized through floral art, celebratory vestments, and the use of the finest secondary symbols (see above) the church has in its possession. Easter ends on Pentecost Sunday.

- Ordinary time. The time after Pentecost is characterized by an emphasis on Sunday as the original feast day of the resurrection. This is an especially appropriate time for artists in the church to express their creative talents for the ongoing celebration of the resurrection. (Note that the time between Epiphany and Ash Wednesday, i.e., between the Christmas season and Lent, is also classified as ordinary time.)

CONCLUSION

Worship is the ministry of Christ in his body. He is there to touch people, to heal them, and to make them whole. Everything in the environment of worship is the servant of Christ's action; the environment *serves* the people. Anything that interferes with or hinders the ministry of Christ is out of place.

STUDY GUIDE

Read Session 9, "The Primary Worship Environment,"
before answering these questions.

PART I: PERSONAL STUDY

Answer the following questions on your own.

1. Life Connection

◆ Think about this statement: "We shape our environment, then our environment shapes us." Illustrate this principle from your experience in various worship spaces. _____

_____

_____

_____

_____

2. Content Questions

◆ Summarize the biblical and theological principles regarding environment and worship. Write out the principles on the left. Then, summarize them in your own words on the right.

Principles	My Understanding of Them
1. _____	_____
_____	_____
2. _____	_____
_____	_____
3. _____	_____
_____	_____

◆ Identify and explain the two primary symbols of the worship environment.

a. The body gathered: _____

_____

b. The furniture of worship: _____

_____

◆ In the space below draw a picture of your church interior, locating the primary symbols.

◆ Describe the seating arrangement. Are people able to participate in the worship and relate to each other? _____

_____

_____

_____

_____

◆ Evaluate the people's line of sight. Can they all see the primary symbols?

_____

_____

◆ Summarize how the worship environment may change during the various seasons of the Christian year.

Advent_____

_____

Christmas_____

_____

Epiphany _____

_____

Holy Week _____

_____

Easter _____

_____

Pentecost _____

_____

3. *Application*

♦ If you were asked to change the worship environment of your local church, what would you suggest? Draw your suggestion in the space below:

PART II: GROUP DISCUSSION

Share the insights you gained from your personal study in Part I. Write out all answers that group members give to the questions on a chalkboard, a flip chart, or a dry erase board.

1. *Life Connection*

♦ Begin your discussion by asking group members to discuss their experience of the principle, "We shape our environment, then our environment shapes us."

2. *Thought Questions*

♦ Discuss in order each of the biblical and theological principles regarding the worship environment.

♦ Spend some time sharing various responses to the two primary symbols of the worship environment (the body gathered and the furniture).

♦ Ask all group members to share their pictures of the inside of the church, showing the location of the primary symbols.

- Comment on the arrangement of the people. Does the space foster participation or spectator worship?

- Talk about the line of sight. Can people see the primary symbols? Are the primary symbols aesthetically pleasing?

- Walk through the environment for the seasons of the Christian year. Probe how the environment may change from season to season.

3. *Application*

- Ask various group members to share their conclusions regarding the mandate to change the worship space in their local church. Compare drawings and talk about each person's ideas.

- Discuss the kind of environmental change each person would like to make for each of the seasons of the Christian year.

- How has the study of the primary worship environment enriched and extended your understanding of worship?

THE SECONDARY WORSHIP ENVIRONMENT

A Study in Ceremony

 I have had the privilege of worshiping in nearly all the major church bodies because of my travels. I have experienced worship in the great cathedrals of the world as well as in house churches with small groups of people.

In a plain worship setting the primary symbols of worship are apparent in the people, the pulpit, the table, and usually a font or pool. The debate is not about the primary and necessary furniture of worship, but about the more elaborate ornate environment and the ceremonial.

If your church makes extensive use of visual and ceremonial elements, then I hope this study will enrich your understanding. If your church delights in plainness, I hope this session will give you a better appreciation of those who employ ceremony in their worship.

The following secondary symbols which are the concern of this session have been used in various churches over the years.

TABLE (ALTAR) HANGINGS

In the early church, cloths were probably not placed on the Lord's Table. However, there is evidence that in the third century a silk cloth covered it. By the fourth century, Christians began to decorate the cloth with embroidery and jewels, so much so that John Chrysostom, a bishop of Constantinople, warned against paying too much attention to the cloth. Over the decorated cloth another linen cloth was placed for the celebration of the Eucharist. In the medieval era this top cloth was replaced by a frontal cloth that hung down the front of the altar (now placed against the back wall of the church). In renewed practice today the Lord's Table is either left bare or covered with an inconspicuous cloth. Elaborate cloths are shunned, since they tend to call attention to themselves and detract from the bread and wine, the dominant visual symbols of the action taking place at the table.

In traditions where the table is set with bread and Communion dishes holding the individual cups, a cloth covers the elements until the service at the table begins. Many churches are eliminating the cloth—its appearance suggests a covered body. By allowing the elements to be seen, the image of the resurrection is communicated. This symbol is in keeping with the emphasis on the presence of the risen Lord at the table.

BANNERS

The use of banners to communicate ideas and create feelings antedates Old Testament times. The armies of the Egyptians, the Persians, and the Assyrians used banners. The various tribes of Israel adopted them as well (Num 2:2). In medieval times, simple folk made bright tapestries of wool, linen, and silk embellished with gold threads for use in worship. In modern times, banners have been rediscovered and revived for use in worship.

There are three basic rules to keep in mind about the use of banners in worship. First, they are not decorations. A banner is not a piece of artwork that is placed somewhere in the church to add color or serve some aesthetic purpose. Second, a banner should say something about what is happening in the specific worship service in which it appears. Third, banners have a limited use and are not to be thought of as permanent fixtures in a worship setting. A banner associated with a season such as Advent or Lent could be hung on the wall during that season, or it could be used for the entrance procession, then placed in a stand during worship and used again in the recessional.

If we follow these three rules, banners will retain their function as servants of the word. If we choose to decorate our worship space with many ceiling and wall banners, we will find that their presence overpowers the primary symbols; they will clutter the space and detract from the main focus of worship with too many messages.

CANDLES

The significance of candles in worship relates to the light they project. Christ is the light of the world, and the light of the candle speaks this truth. The entire body of worshipers may carry numerous candles in processions, particularly in services that celebrate the birth or resurrection of Christ.

There are no universal rules about the use of candles in worship. Each congregation may determine its own use, keeping in mind that candles are reminders of Christ, the light of the world, not mere decorations.

CHALICE AND PATEN

The chalice is the cup that holds wine, symbolizing the blood of Christ shed for the forgiveness of sin; the paten is the dish that holds bread, symbolizing the body of Christ broken for our salvation. These liturgical utensils have been the object of considerable artistic attention throughout history because of their functional importance.

After the Reformation many Protestant churches introduced individual cups in place of the chalice. Today many churches are returning to the chalice or are using both chalice and individual cups. Where individual cups are used, the dish that holds them is usually made of pewter or silver and serves the symbol well. The use of plastic cups instead of glass cups poses a problem. Plastic does not serve well the importance of Christ's shed blood. It tends to cheapen the symbol and detract from its importance. If the individual cups are retained, it is advisable to return to the glass cups even though considerable time is spent in cleaning them.

COLOR IN WORSHIP

Through the centuries, certain colors have taken on meanings that serve the seasons of the Christian year. The use of color in worship is rooted not in any biblical precedent but in developments in the medieval era. For the first thousand years of the church, vestments were usually white, and color was used indiscriminately in the church. During the twelfth century colors were organized according to different seasons and various festivals. By the early thirteenth century, Pope Innocent III ruled that white is for feast days, red for martyrs' days, and black for penitential seasons.

Today various colors are used to correspond with the seasons:

◆ Advent: Royal blue or purple. Royal blue is a kingly color representing the second coming of Christ the King, and purple is the color of repentance.

◆ Christmas: White or gold. These are colors for festive occasions.

◆ After Epiphany: Green. This is the color for ordinary time and signifies continuity.

- Lent: Purple for penitence.
- Holy Week: Black for sobriety.
- Easter: White and gold for festivity.
- Pentecost: Red for the martyrs of the church.
- After Pentecost: Green for continuity.

Colors are also used for specific occasions:
- Baptism: White or red
- Confirmation: White or red
- Ordination: White
- Marriage: White
- Funeral: Violet, blue, or black
- Dedication of a church: White

Colors may be used in vestments, pulpit hangings, table cloths, and banners.

Cross

A variety of crosses appear in many churches—Orthodox, Catholic, and Protestant. The use of the cross as a visual symbol has a complicated history. An empty cross symbolizing the resurrection was used very early. Processional crosses were used as early as the fourth century. A church should not allow a cross to become the dominant symbol, overpowering the primary symbols. The design and material of the cross should compliment the primary symbols of pulpit, table, and font (or pool). When used in a processional, a cross is placed in a stand next to the table and used again to lead the recessional.

Glass

Stained-glass windows originated in the medieval period. Their original purpose was to tell a story, show the deeds of a biblical character, or proclaim a message, such as the judgment.

In contemporary worship renewal, glass has a place as long as it does not call attention to itself. It should create a mood, not a distraction. It should speak to the unconscious mind, not the conscious mind. It should assist the gospel and the primary symbols by evoking feelings of joy and wonder, trust and love. The true function of glass is to create an atmosphere in which the worshiper senses the power of God's love and transcendence.

The Puritans, on the other hand, preferred clear glass for church windows. They wanted to make the point that worship is not a retreat into a different, sacred reality, as stained glass can suggest; rather, it remains in contact with the everyday world, which is the sphere in which God's saving grace operates. Some contemporary churches follow the Puritan practice.

LITURGICAL BOOKS

In the medieval era it became customary to adorn the books from which the services were read, especially the Gospel book, with symbols of beauty, such as pictures set among jewels.

In contemporary worship renewal, artistic attention is being paid again to books used in worship. The emphasis is on simplicity of design so that the books do not become objects of attention, but objects that serve the gospel by creating an atmosphere of respect.

PROJECTION AND LIGHTING TECHNIQUES

Slide projectors, overhead projectors, and various lighting techniques can be used to create "projected environments" for a particular occasion of worship. Various images can be projected onto walls, ceilings, or screens to trigger the imagination. Because this kind of visual imagery can become an end in itself, overpowering the more subtle communication of the primary symbols of pulpit, table, and font, it is important to use these technologies sparingly.

VESTMENTS

Vestments, the clothing worn by the worship celebrants, began to become distinct from ordinary clothing in the fourth and fifth centuries. During the first three centuries of Christianity the celebrant wore the civilian dress of the Roman Empire: the alb, stole, and chasuble. During the fourth and fifth centuries, Roman dress changed under the influence of the barbarians, who introduced trousers and shirts. However, the celebrants of worship retained Roman dress. The consequent differentiation resulted in a distinct clerical dress for worship.

Most Protestants rejected vestments. But as a result of the twentieth century renewal, many churches are returning to the ancient use of the simple alb, stole, and chasuble.

CONCLUSION

Visual art never exists as an end in itself in worship. The celebration of the gospel, which takes place at the pulpit, the table, and sometimes the font, is of first importance. These primary symbols are served by many secondary symbols, whose function is always to signify the primary action or to assist this action. It is important to plan the use of secondary symbols carefully, lest they overpower the primary symbols and thus function in a negative rather than a positive way.

STUDY GUIDE

Read Session 10, "The Secondary Worship Environment,"
before answering these questions.

PART I: PERSONAL STUDY

Answer the following questions on your own.

1. *Life Connection*

- Recall an experience of worshiping in a church that made elaborate use of ceremony. _____

_____

_____

_____

2. *Content Questions*

- In your owns words, define a secondary symbol. _____

_____

_____

_____

_____

- Read Exodus 36:8–38. How would you describe the use of visual arts in the tabernacle? Draw a picture of it or find one in a Bible or Bible dictionary.

◆ Why has the contemporary church rejected the use of the elaborate cloth that used to cover the eucharistic table? _____

_____

_____

_____

_____

◆ Read Numbers 2:2. How was the banner used in ancient Israel?

_____

_____

_____

_____

◆ What are the three basic rules to keep in mind regarding the use of banners in worship?

a. _____

_____

b. _____

_____

c. _____

_____

◆ Read John 1:1–9. List all the characteristics of light that are set forth in this passage. _____

_____

_____

_____

_____

_____

◆ How may a candle be used in worship? _____

_____

_____

_____

_____

_____

◆ Read Matthew 26:26–30. Why do you think the ornamental cup (chalice) has had such a significant history in the church? _____

_____

_____

_____

_____

◆ Color has also had an important place in the history of worship. The colors of banners, pulpit hangings, table cloths, and vestments change from season to season to represent the theme of each Christian season as it relates to God's work of salvation. In the space below state the color of each season and the reason for the color. Use the appropriate columns for your answer.

Season	Color	Reason for Color
Advent	_____	_____
Christmas	_____	_____
Epiphany	_____	_____
Lent	_____	_____
Holy Week	_____	_____
Easter	_____	_____
Pentecost	_____	_____

◆ Why has the cross gained so much importance as a visual symbol in worship? _____

_____

_____

_____

_____

◆ How should a cross be used in worship? _____

_____

_____

_____

_____

• Have you ever been in a church with an oversized cross? Has it detracted from the primary symbols of pulpit and table? Explain. _____

_____

_____

_____

• What was the original purpose of stained-glass windows?

_____

_____

_____

_____

• What is the general use of glass in contemporary churches?

_____

_____

_____

_____

_____

• Why did it become a custom to adorn the Gospel book?

_____

_____

_____

_____

_____

• How is the Gospel book adorned in contemporary worship?

_____

_____

_____

_____

• Describe a "projected environment." _____

_____

_____

_____

_____

◆ How did distinctive vestments come to be used?_____

_____

_____

_____

_____

◆ What is the role of a secondary symbol in worship?_____

_____

_____

_____

_____

PART II: GROUP DISCUSSION

Share the insights you gained from your personal study in Part I. Write out all answers that group members give to the questions on a chalkboard, a flip chart, or a dry erase board.

1. *Life Connection*

◆ Begin your discussion by asking various group members to recount their experiences with elaborate ceremony in church. Be sure to ask them about their emotional response to the ceremony. Was worship cluttered? Were the secondary symbols used as servants of the primary action of worship?

2. *Thought Questions*

◆ Read Exodus 36:8–38. Compare group members' insights. Ask, How does what is described in Exodus serve the primary act of coming before God?

◆ Discuss whether your church should cover the eucharistic elements of bread and wine with a cloth.

◆ How have banners been used in the church? Evaluate the use of banners in your worship. Do you follow the three basic rules regarding the use of banners?

◆ Read John 1:1–9. Discuss the image of light in the New Testament. How should you use candles in your worship?

- Read Matthew 26:26–30. Ask, What is the importance of the cup? How should the history of the chalice influence your concern for aesthetic Communion ware?

- Review the color for each season of the Christian year and explore the relationship of that color to the meaning of the season. Ask, Does the color correspond in your mind to the meaning of the season?

- How is a cross used in your worship? Is any change needed?

- How is glass used in your church? If you have stained-glass windows, it might be helpful to examine several of them for their meaning.

- Describe the book from which you read your Scripture lessons. Should your church purchase a new book?

- Do you use a "projected environment" during worship? If so, does it dominate the primary symbols of pulpit and table? Ask, How could a projected environment be integrated into our worship?

- Discuss the pros and cons of wearing vestments in worship.

3. *Application*
- Spend some time making a list of all the secondary environmental symbols in your worship space.

- Evaluate each secondary symbol in relation to the primary symbols of pulpit, table, and font or pool (if visible). Ask, Is the secondary symbol interpreted appropriately, or does it dominate a primary symbol?

- What value have you found in studying secondary symbols. How has it enriched your understanding of worship?

DRAMA IN WORSHIP

A Study in Medium as Message

 Today we are returning to a form of communication that emphasizes the visual and the dramatic. Interestingly, the medieval era was also a time of visual and dramatic communication. I have seen some good drama in worship that really communicated God's word, but I have also seen some very poor drama that overpowered the word and called attention to itself. Good drama always serves the word and never interferes with the word by obscuring or distorting it. But poor drama overpowers the word.

DRAMA IN OLD TESTAMENT WORSHIP

Hebrew worship, beginning with the early sacrifices made by Abel and his successors—Abraham, the patriarchs, and the priesthood of Israel—is a dramatic portrayal of the relationship that men and women have with God. The sacrifices of the Old Testament follow a common pattern that constitutes a powerful four-part drama. First, the worshipers went through an extensive preparation and personal cleansing that was followed by a ritual of preparing an animal for slaughter. Second, in a ceremonial rite the animal was offered as a gift to God, who is the giver of all gifts. Third, the animal was butchered and certain parts were burned on the altar. Fourth, both priest and people shared a great feast together with God as they ate the animal that had been offered. In this dramatic action the stuff of everyday life, which came from God, was offered to God, and was then returned by God to the people for the feast in which God shared. In this drama the true meaning of life was portrayed in a powerful four-act play.

This sense of dramatizing a relationship to God has a central place in all the Jewish feasts. The Sabbath is a dramatic remembrance of God's creative act; Passover, a reenactment of the exodus; Shavuoth (the Feast of Weeks), a celebration of the harvest; Rosh Hashanah (the Feast of Trumpets), a drama of the new year;

Yom Kippur (the Day of Atonement), a drama of returning to God; Sukkoth (the Feast of Tabernacles or Booths), a dramatic remembrance that Israel lived in huts (booths) when God called them up out of Egypt. In all of these celebrations Israel told and acted out the story of how God had met them. Drama was the underlying structure of worship.

DRAMA IN NEW TESTAMENT WORSHIP

The same approach to worship is found in New Testament times. The service of the word is a dramatic retelling of God's great acts of creation, the fall, the patriarchs, the exodus, the conquest of Canaan, the prophets, the coming of Jesus and his birth, life, death, resurrection, ascension, and coming again. This is story and drama at its best, a play about the meaning of the world and of our lives within world history.

Furthermore, the Eucharist (Lord's Supper) is the great drama of God's saving act in Jesus Christ. (The connection between the dramatic feasts of the Old Testament and the eucharistic drama and feast of Christian worship is more than coincidental.) The drama of redemption is acted out and symbolized in the taking, blessing, breaking, and giving of bread and wine. This drama has an affinity with eating and drinking at home, with the drama of life continually nourished. It is a dramatic reenactment of the most important event in history, the event through which a new creation was birthed, the event that marks the beginning of the steady march of creation toward becoming the new heavens and the new earth. It is not to be taken lightly.

Among Christians, drama soon fell on hard times. The church fathers rejected it, but it made a comeback in the medieval era. The Reformers, including modern Protestants, largely ignored its place in worship. But today drama is making a significant comeback in worship renewal.

DRAMA IN WORSHIP TODAY

Drama has come full circle in the twentieth century. The dramatic nature of every service of worship, the dramatic character of the great festivals of the church year, and the inclusion of small dramas in worship are all matters of interest. Generally, three criteria are used to measure the dramatic character of these services: (1) the emotional and physical involvement of the congregation, (2) the presence of crisis and conflict in the drama, and (3) the reenactment of an important spiritual experience or the rehearsal of something that is to be performed in the world.

Certain forms of drama are inappropriate in worship. Yet they may be appropriate in educational situations such as Sunday school, in recreational situations such as church parties, or in family worship. Youth plays, drama games, skits, puppets, clowns, and parades are all forms of drama that are useful means of communicating truth, but are not generally acceptable in a morning worship of word and table. Because the great drama of the Christian faith is expressed primarily through word and table, the use of small dramas must always serve these two focal points and never replace them or even overshadow them. Consequently, renewalists recommend forms of drama such as choral reading, storytelling, and chancel drama in a worship service. These are especially useful in the service of the word, where they heighten important aspects of the scriptural text.

VARIOUS KINDS OF DRAMA

Many different kinds of drama are being used in the church today. A listing of some of these with a brief description of each will give you a sense of the breadth of this art form.

- Festival music drama. The festival music drama, generally associated with large churches, is usually presented at Christmas and Easter. Many new dramas have been produced in recent years and range from children's dramas to huge Hollywood-style productions. These dramas usually represent some aspect of God's saving work and also pursue the purpose of evangelism.

- Readers' theater. Readers' theater attempts to present a Scripture text rather than a saving event. It may be presented during worship as a Scripture reading. Often the reading is associated with the celebration of a saving event in one or another of the seasons of the Christian year.

- Chancel drama. Chancel drama is usually associated with a Scripture text. A group of players may dramatize a Scripture passage rather than read it.

- Storytelling. Storytelling is a narrative form of drama in which the storyteller tells the gospel story as an eyewitness. Storytelling can be used at any time but is probably most effective at Christmas and Easter.

◆ Sermon setup. Many contemporary churches prepare a very brief drama to set the stage for the sermon. It is usually a secular drama that deals with life issues presented in the sermon. Willow Creek Church in Barrington, Illinois, has pioneered this form of drama.

DRAMA DURING THE CHRISTIAN YEAR

While drama may be effective on any Sunday, it is most useful during the special seasons of the Christian year when we celebrate God's saving events in history. Drama can be used to express the following themes:

◆ Advent: The coming of Christ at Bethlehem, in our hearts, and at the end of history (prophetic literature)

◆ Christmas: The birth of Christ (opening chapters of the Gospels)

◆ Epiphany: The manifestation of Jesus as the Messiah and the Savior of the world (the wise men, the baptism, the miracles)

◆ Lent: The teachings of Jesus and the growing opposition from the religious leaders (the Gospels)

◆ Holy Week: The final intense days of Jesus, particularly Palm Sunday, Maundy Thursday, Good Friday (the Gospels)

◆ Easter: The resurrection and postresurrection experiences; the ascension (the Gospels)

◆ Pentecost: The coming of the Holy Spirit (Acts 2)

CONCLUSION

Drama in worship mobilizes the people in your church who have the gift of communication. You may want to form a lay readers' group for the purpose of bringing the communicators together to use their gifts in worship. Drama used thoughtfully and prayerfully can be a positive form of communication in the worship of your church.

STUDY GUIDE

Read Session 11, "Drama in Worship,"
before answering these questions.

PART I: PERSONAL STUDY

Answer the following questions on your own.

1. *Life Connection*

◆ Recall an experience of drama in worship. Evaluate it below. Did it serve the word or did it overpower the word? _____

_____

_____

_____

2. *Content Questions*

◆ Outline and explain in your own words the drama of making a sacrifice in the Old Testament.

The Steps of the Sacrifice   Their Meaning

a. _____   _____

    _____   _____

b. _____   _____

    _____   _____

c. _____   _____

    _____   _____

d. _____   _____

    _____   _____

◆ Read Exodus 12 and list all the dramatic actions that gave shape to the Passover celebration. _____

_____

_____

_____

◆ What historical event does each Jewish feast dramatize?

Sabbath _____

_____

Passover _____

_____

Feast of Weeks _____

_____

Rosh Hashanah _____

_____

Yom Kippur _____

_____

Feast of Tabernacles _____

_____

◆ Explain how the service of the word in worship is characterized by an underlying drama. _____

_____

_____

◆ Explain how the Eucharist is characterized by an underlying drama.

_____

_____

_____

◆ Why do you suppose drama is making a comeback in today's church?

_____

_____

_____

◆ What three criteria are used to judge drama in the church?

a. _____

_____

b. _____

_____

c. _____

_____

◆ List and explain the various themes from which drama may be developed in the seasons of the Christian year.

Advent _____

Christmas _____

Epiphany _____

Lent _____

Holy Week _____

Easter _____

Pentecost _____

3. *Application*

◆ Prepare a drama to be used in your church. Draw on the Gospel accounts or create a sermon setup drama. If you don't have time to develop a drama, choose a passage or theme you would like to see dramatized.

PART II: GROUP DISCUSSION

Share the insights you gained from your personal study in Part I. Write out all answers that group members give to the questions on a chalkboard, a flip chart, or a dry erase board.

1. *Life Connection*

◆ Begin your study by asking several members of the group to share their experiences of drama in worship. Explore whether the drama met the criteria of good drama in worship.

◆ Discuss how you would decide which drama belongs in worship and which belongs in other gatherings of the church.

◆ Ask the group to name and explain the various kinds of drama that may be used in the worship of the church. List their answers on the chalkboard, flip chart, or dry erase board.

2. *Thought Questions*

◆ Have several people in the group set out the drama of the Old Testament sacrifice.

- Discuss how the drama itself expresses an approach to a relationship with God.

- Read Exodus 12 and discuss the dramatic elements in it.

- Review how each Jewish festival is a drama in its own right.

- Discuss how the service of the word is characterized by an underlying dramatic structure.

- Discuss how the service of the Eucharist is characterized by an underlying dramatic structure.

- Ask several members of the group to give reasons why they think drama is making a comeback in today's church.

- Review the criteria used to judge drama in worship. Ask, What do you think of each of these criteria?

- Review the different kinds of dramas that may be used in the worship of the church.

- Review the different dramatic names for the Christian year.

3. *Application Questions*

- Evaluate the present dramatic nature of both the service of the word and the service of the table in the worship of your church.

- Discuss the dramas that were written or suggested by various members of the group.

- How has this study improved your understanding of the place and use of drama in the church?

DANCE IN WORSHIP

A Study in Worship Movement

Let me tell you about two experiences of dance in worship. The first took place at a festive worship occasion within a traditional church. As clergy and choir processed forward to take their places, they were led by a person carrying the cross high and triumphantly and by a dancer who moved creatively to the tune of the classic hymn being sung. I had to strain to see the dancer, but I was aware of her presence and her movement, which helped to create within me the sense that I, along with a thousand other people, was moving joyfully into the presence of God.

The second experience occurred not long ago in a church where a young person danced to the Lord's Prayer as part of the "worship program." No one sang, we just watched. It was an excellent performance, and everyone burst into appreciative applause when the young person finished.

There is, of course, a significant difference between these two experiences. The one dance served the act of coming before God and so helped me in my own experience of coming into God's presence. The other dance was a performance. It was enjoyable, but it did not serve the action of worship. It was an interlude, an act between other acts of the program, with no apparent purpose other than being that person's performance before God.

Let's look at dance in worship and focus on dance that serves the text, dance that accompanies the flow of worship and is not an isolated event placed willy-nilly in the middle of a program.

DANCE IN BIBLICAL AND HISTORICAL TIMES

The most famous biblical dance was performed by David, who danced with joy in the presence of God as the ark of the Lord entered the city (2 Sam 6:12–15). Other examples include the dance of Miriam and the prophetesses who danced with tambourines in response to their deliverance from the pursuing Egyptian army (Exod 15:20) and the women who danced at the Shiloh feast (Judg 21:21–23).

In the Old Testament we also find exhortations to dance, such as "let them praise his name with dancing" (Ps 149:3) and "praise him with tambourine and dancing" (Ps 150:4).

There is no clear support for dancing in the New Testament. Dance may have been performed in the early church, as suggested by Ambrose, who admonished Christians in the fourth century with these words: "He who dances as David dances, dances in grace." Dance appears in the medieval era, primarily in city and village festivals. While dance was certainly not used by the Reformation church, Renaissance painters such as Leonardo da Vinci pictured dancing in heaven and saw the whole creation ablaze with dance. During the modern period, dance has been performed in the church only by the Shaker movement (eighteenth century) and some nineteenth-century communities.

In modern worship renewal, both liturgical and charismatic, there has been a significant revival of dance. This dance has accompanied the renewal of the heart and spirit. There seems to be a link between the restoration of faith and the joy of being renewed.

APPROPRIATE DANCE IN WORSHIP

My opening illustration demonstrated the difference between appropriate and inappropriate dance in worship. Let's look at some forms of dance that are quite appropriate for worship in the local church.

- ◆ Worship movements. Common worship movements include special bodily postures such as standing, kneeling, raising hands, genuflecting, or making the sign of the cross. (These movements would not usually be thought of as dance, but we may extend the concept of dance to encompass all such symbolic movement.)

- ◆ Movement of the entire community. In many churches people stand together, walk the aisle to receive Christ, walk the aisle to receive bread and wine. In many charismatic and praise and worship churches entire congregations move to music, raise hands together, and form circles of prayer. All of these are a kind of dance.

- ◆ Accompaniment dance. As described in my opening illustration, a dancer may lead processions and recessions. Accompaniment dance may also occur in conjunction with a Scripture reading. I once experienced a reading of the raising of Lazarus accompanied by a group of dancers who acted out the story as it was being read. The dance was subtle and underplayed so it acted as an assist in the reading of Scripture. It was a powerful experience of God's truth.

DANCE SERVES THE TEXT

Because dance is not a performance or a program, but an accompaniment to a worship action, dance needs to be placed within worship at those points where it serves the text. There are five such points within worship.

- Processional dance. A dancer may accompany processions, recessions, and such actions as the bringing forth of the Gospel to be read or the bringing of the gifts of bread and wine to the table. These are all joyful events in worship whose meaning can be expressed in joyful dance.

- Proclamation dance. This kind of dance accompanies the reading of God's word. It interprets and proclaims the meaning of the Scripture lesson.

- Prayer dance. Certain worship prayers, such as confessions, the sanctus, or doxologies, can be expressed in dance.

- Meditation dance. A meditation dance may accompany the reflective moments of worship such as the reading of a psalm, the silence after a sermon, or a quiet time after communion.

- Celebration dance. Celebration dances usually occur with the prelude or postlude. Sometimes, especially during the postlude, the entire congregation may become involved in movement.

DANCE DURING THE CHRISTIAN YEAR

Dance has always been associated with festive occasions. While every Sunday is a festive celebration of the death and resurrection of Jesus, the Christian year, with its celebration of the particular events of salvation, provides the church with special opportunities for dance. Dance during the Christian year varies in mood from sadness to great joy and celebration. Consider the following summary in thinking about the kind of dance appropriate for services of each season.

- Advent: The mood is a mixture of repentance and joy as the church anticipates the first and second comings of Jesus.

- Christmas: The mood is one of great joy as the church celebrates the incarnation.

- Epiphany: The mood is one of faith response as the church remembers Jesus' manifestation as the Savior of the world.

- Lent: The mood is sober as the church begins to travel the road with Jesus culminating in his rejection at the hands of the religious leaders of his day.

- Holy Week: The mood is grim as Jesus experiences the final episodes of his life, which culminate in death on the cross.

- Easter: The mood is exuberant as Jesus' resurrection from the dead is experienced and celebrated.

- Pentecost: The mood is one of empowerment as the disciples and others receive the Holy Spirit.

CONCLUSION

While the experience of dance may be unfamiliar to most congregations, I urge you to give dance careful attention and thought. It's probably better to proceed cautiously in regard to dance than to rush ahead and be misunderstood.

STUDY GUIDE

Read Session 12, "Dance in Worship,"
before answering these questions.

PART I: PERSONAL STUDY

Answer the following questions on your own.

1. *Life Connection*

♦ Have you experienced dance in worship? If so, describe the dance. Also describe your response to the dance. _____

_____

_____

_____

_____

_____

2. *Content Questions*

♦ Read the record of the following dances described in the Old Testament. Imagine you were there. What would have been your response?

2 Samuel 6:12–15: the dance of David _____

_____

_____

_____

_____

Exodus 15:20: the dance in response to deliverance from the Egyptian army _____

_____

_____

_____

◆ Briefly summarize the history of dance in the church.

Early church _____

_____

Medieval church _____

_____

Reformation and Renaissance era _____

_____

Modern times _____

_____

Contemporary church _____

_____

◆ Briefly describe in your own words the different kinds of dance or dance movements that may be used in the church.

a. Worship movements _____

_____

b. Movement of the entire community _____

_____

c. Accompaniment dance _____

_____

◆ Briefly summarize how the following accompaniment dances may be used in the church.

a. Processional dance _____

_____

b. Proclamation dance _____

_____

c. Prayer dance _____

_____

d. Meditation dance _____

_____

e. Celebration dance _____

_____

- In the space below summarize the mood of each season of the Christian year and comment on how this mood may shape the experience of worship dance for each season.

Advent _____

_____

Christmas _____

_____

Epiphany _____

_____

Lent _____

_____

Holy Week _____

_____

Easter _____

_____

Pentecost _____

_____

3. *Application*
- Choose a passage of Scripture that you would like to see danced in the worship of your church.

PART II: GROUP DISCUSSION

Share the insights you gained from your personal study in Part I. Write out all answers that group members give to the questions on a chalkboard, a flip chart, or a dry erase board.

1. *Life Connection*
- Begin your discussion by asking members of the group to describe their experience of dance in worship.

2. *Thought Questions*
- Read 2 Samuel 6:12–15 and ask group members to respond to this experience of dance. How would they have felt if they had been there?

- Read Exodus 15:22 and ask the group to respond to this experience of dance. How would they have felt if they had been there?

- Gain a perspective of the history of dance in worship by discussing the brief summary made by each person. You may want to make a timeline and write it on the board. Does history teach us anything about the use of dance in worship?

- Summarize the movements that are made in worship. Ask, Do you think of the movements we make during worship as a kind of dance?

- Evaluate the different kinds of accompaniment dance used in the church. Would you like to see one or more of these used in your church?

- Discuss the mood of each season of the Christian year. What kind of dance (community or accompaniment) would best express the mood of each season?

3. *Application*

- Evaluate the present state of dance in your church (the movements used by the entire congregation). What does the community experience in each? Evaluate the common movements you currently use in worship.

- If you have used accompaniment dance in your worship, evaluate its effectiveness.

- Plan an accompaniment dance for your worship. What kind would you use? Where would you place it?

- How has this session helped you better understand the place and use of dance in worship?

THE ARTS IN THE FUTURE OF CHRISTIAN WORSHIP

A Study in Future Worship Trends

 The arts have made significant inroads into the worship of many churches, and I think it's safe to say that the arts have a bright future in worship, especially in the following traditions.

- ◆ The liturgical tradition. I have been in liturgical churches where the ceremony of worship has been graced by the dignified use of the arts. While liturgical churches have always used the arts, the increased number of artists and artistic guilds within the liturgical church suggests a strong future.

- ◆ The free church tradition (nonliturgical Protestants). Historically the free church tradition neglected the arts in worship. Free church Christians considered themselves people of the book, not of ceremony. Worship meant gathering around the book, focusing on the book, and doing nothing that would detract from the book. Today Protestants of the free church tradition are rediscovering the place of the arts in worship, without detracting from the centrality of the book.

- ◆ The charismatic tradition. Charismatics are strongly associated with dance, particularly community dance. There is among them a growing interest in drama and the environmental arts as well.

Considering these trends, the outlook for the arts in worship seems quite favorable. In this final session let's look at the arts in worship, first from the perspective of the space in which we worship, and second in terms of the various uses of the arts in the fourfold pattern of worship.

THE SPACE IN WHICH WE WORSHIP

In Session 9 we identified the primary symbols of worship as God's people gathered in a space to celebrate God's saving events through word and table.

Worship renewalists are reexamining the space in which worship takes place—how the space is arranged, how the people are seated, where the pulpit and table are situated. All of these concerns are directed toward communicating with God and with each other.

Unfortunately the space in most of our churches works against worship renewal. People are seated for a program to watch, not an action in which they are called to participate. Congregational participation lies at the heart of worship renewal. If we are to participate with each other in the action of worship, we need a space that encourages and releases engagement, involvement, and participation.

SPACE IN A RENEWAL CHURCH

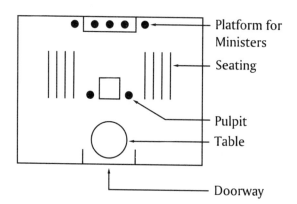

The church pictured above viewed the restoration of participation as a high priority. It followed the ancient Christian pattern of separate spaces for the two prominent acts of worship. Note that the eucharistic table and the place for the service of the word are separate spaces. Consequently the congregation had to move from one space to the other. The acts of gathering occurred as people gathered and stood in a circle around the table. They sang a hymn as they moved to the service of the word space for the Scripture readings, the sermon, and response. After the service of the word, they sang another hymn as they made their way to the eucharistic table where they stood for Communion and remained standing for the dismissal.

I'm not assuming that you will gut your church and completely remodel it. This diagram represents a worship space for a church of about 100–150 people, a number small enough that the designers could opt for intimacy and relationship in their space. I have given you this example to stimulate thought and action regarding a worship that is participatory and intimate. The church is the family of God, a community. That needs to be experienced as a context for better worship.

Now let's turn to a possible scenario for the arts in worship.

THE GATHERING

A primary concern of the gathering is to welcome worshipers into the presence of God. The arts may be used to express the hospitality of God's people. The act of a handshake, a smile, a courteous seating symbolizes hospitality.

The major art form of the gathering is the procession, which symbolizes the people's movement into the presence of God. The procession may be led with a cross (Christ leads the way), a banner (proclaiming the name of the day), or a dancer (expressing joy). Processions are making a comeback. When they work, they express great joy. They make use of color, festive music, and dramatic movement to convey the importance of coming before God.

THE SERVICE OF THE WORD

The service of the word primarily communicates the word of God, so the renewal of communication arts can find a happy home in the spoken word of worship. Priorities for the future include learning to read the Scripture well, increasing the use of drama (particularly during the seasons of the Christian year), storytelling the gospel, and maintaining strong preaching.

THE SERVICE OF THE EUCHARIST

The Eucharist is primarily a response to the word. The heart of the Eucharist is to give thanks and to offer praise to the triune God. A drama in its own right, it enacts the dying and rising of Christ. New attention will be paid to the Eucharist. Its celebration will increase among Protestants; the fullness of its historic prayers will be recovered; songs and choruses of substance and meaning will find a home in the Communion song; the movement of the people to bring the bread and wine will be recovered and take on a new dignity. The minister will learn to use dramatic gesture and tone of voice. The people will be more inclined to move forward to receive bread and wine and to express reverence in their physical and spiritual posture.

THE ALTERNATIVE FORM OF THANKSGIVING

This alternative to the celebration of the Eucharist is a new emphasis, particularly among those who wish to follow the ancient fourfold pattern of worship. It will serve as a precursor to more frequent celebration of Communion.

Because it constitutes a collaborative response to God's work of salvation and to the working of God in the lives of the people now, it is a natural home for the arts. Artistic response will find a place here. People may bring their art as an offering of praise. They may offer the work of their hands—banners, metal symbols, painting, dance, as well as a host of individual gifts—to God as an act of praise.

THE SERVICE OF DISMISSAL

The dismissal is a good-bye that sends people forth. It will remain short. The primary art form of the dismissal will be a joyous recessional in which the leaders of worship, and in some cases the congregation itself, recesses with dramatic movement and art objects (books, crosses, banners) into the world to love and serve the Lord.

THE ARTS IN THE CHRISTIAN YEAR

The Christian year, with its reenactment of the saving deeds of God in Christ, affords wonderful opportunities for the arts. A summary of the events of salvation we celebrate in the Christian year is listed below. Use this summary to think about the use of the environmental arts as well as music, drama, and dance.

- Advent: Preannouncements of the coming of Christ
- Christmas: The fulfillment of the hope of Israel in the birth of the Messiah
- Epiphany: The announcement and manifestation of Christ as the Savior of the whole world as well as the Messiah of Israel
- Lent: Preparation for the death of Christ
- Holy Week: Entrance into the passion and death of Jesus
- Easter: Joyful participation in the resurrection
- Pentecost: Openness to the presence of the Holy Spirit

Conclusion

No one can predict the future with accuracy, but if present trends continue, the next generation of Christians will make even more effective use of the arts in worship.

STUDY GUIDE

Read Session 13, "The Arts in the Future of Christian Worship,"
before answering these questions.

PART I: PERSONAL STUDY

Answer the following questions on your own.

1. Life Connection

◆ Describe your experience of the use of the arts in one or more of the following traditions: liturgical, free church, charismatic. If you have had experience in more than one of these traditions, describe how they differ.

_____

_____

_____

_____

_____

2. Content Questions

◆ How is space used in the service of the word and in Communion in your church? Is there a noticeable difference? _____

_____

_____

_____

◆ Explain how you respond to the use of space that was described in this study. _____

_____

_____

_____

◆ How would you use the space in your church differently?_____

_____

_____

_____

• If you were to redesign the worship space of your church, what would it look like? Draw it below.

• How may the arts be used in the gathering of the people for worship?

_____

_____

_____

_____

• How may the arts be used in the service of the word?

_____

_____

_____

_____

• How may the arts be used in the service of Communion?

_____

_____

_____

_____

• How may the arts be used in the alternative service of thanksgiving?

_____

_____

_____

_____

◆ How may the arts be used in the dismissal? _____

_____

_____

_____

_____

_____

_____

◆ Use the following space to summarize how you would use the arts in the Christian year.

Season	Environmental Arts	Drama	Dance
Advent	_____	_____	_____
	_____	_____	_____
Christmas	_____	_____	_____
	_____	_____	_____
Epiphany	_____	_____	_____
	_____	_____	_____
Lent	_____	_____	_____
	_____	_____	_____
Holy Week	_____	_____	_____
	_____	_____	_____
Easter	_____	_____	_____
	_____	_____	_____
Pentecost	_____	_____	_____
	_____	_____	_____

3. *Application*

◆ Choose at least one season of the Christian year and outline below how you would use environmental art, the dramatic arts, and dance in the services of that season.

Season _____

_____

Environmental art _____

_____

Drama _____

_____

Dance _____

_____

PART II: GROUP DISCUSSION

Share the insights you gained from your personal study in Part I. Write out all answers that group members give to the questions on a chalkboard, a flip chart, or a dry erase board.

1. *Life Connection*

◆ Begin your discussion by inviting people to comment on their experience of the arts in liturgical, free church, and charismatic worship. What are the differences?

2. *Thought Questions*

◆ Discuss the use of space in the church described in this session.

◆ Ask various group members to share their pictures of the redesigned space in your church. Ask them to give reasons for the changes they have made.

◆ Discuss how the arts may be used in the fourfold pattern of worship: the gathering, the service of the word, the service of Eucharist or the alternative service of thanksgiving, the service of dismissal.

◆ Discuss how the arts may be used in each of the seasons of the Christian year: Advent, Christmas, Epiphany, Lent, Holy Week, Easter, Pentecost.

3. *Application*

- Plan a worship service that includes appropriate use of the arts.
- Plan the use of the arts for one worship service of one season of the Christian year.
- What has this course taught you about the use of music and the other arts in worship?